HOW TO START AND RUN YOUR OWN
RESTAURANT

If you want to know how ...

Going for Self-Employment

Enjoy the sense of achievement and satisfaction that comes from being your own boss

Book-keeping & Accounting for the Small Business

How to keep the books and maintain financial control over your business

The Small Business Start-Up Workbook

A step-by-step guide to starting the business you've dreamed of

Preparing a Winning Business Plan

How to win the attention of investors and stakeholders

howtobooks

Please send for a free copy of the latest catalogue to:
How To Books
Spring Hill House, Spring Hill Road, Begbroke,
Oxford OX5 1RX, United Kingdom
email: info@howtobooks.co.uk
www.howtobooks.co.uk

HOW TO START AND RUN YOUR OWN
RESTAURANT

CAROL GODSMARK

howtobooks

Published by How To Books Ltd
Spring Hill House, Spring Hill Road,
Begbroke, Oxford OX5 1RX, United Kingdom.
Tel: (01865) 375794. Fax: (01865) 379162.
info@howtobooks.co.uk
www.howtobooks.co.uk

First edition 2005
Reprinted 2005
Reprinted 2006

British Library Cataloguing in Publication Data
A catalogue record for this book is available from the British
Library

ISBN 13: 978 1 84528 019 2
ISBN 10: 1 84528 019 9

Cover design by Baseline Arts Ltd, Oxford
Illustrations by Nicki Averill
Produced for How To Books by Deer Park Productions,
Tavistock, Devon
Typeset by Pantek Arts Ltd, Maidstone, Kent
Printed and bound in Great Britain by Bell and Bain Ltd, Glasgow

Contents

Acknowledgements

Researching this book has unearthed many enthusiastic, dedicated professional people who have generously contributed their time and expertise and whom I thank most sincerely:

Peter Gordon of Providores, London; Kit Chapman, the Castle Hotel, Taunton, Somerset, and Brazz Restaurants; Jonathan Cooper, Amano Cafe, London; Jake Watkins, JSW, Petersfield, Hampshire; Raymond Blanc and Tracey Clinton, Manoir Aux Quat' Saisons; Laurence Murphy, Fat Olives; Ray Farthing, 36 On The Quay; Chris Allwood, Allwood's Wine Bar; Alistair Gibson, Brookfield Hotel; all of Emsworth, Hampshire; Larry Stone, wine director, Rubicon, San Francisco, California; John Hayler, Planning Department, Chichester District Council; Lawrence Foord and Sarah Parker, Trading Standards, CDC; John White, Environmental Protection, CDC; David Knowles-Ley, Environmental Health, CDC; Julian Mitchell, Christie & Co, London; Brian Duckett and Paul Monaghan, Howarth Franchising, London; Lorna and Peter Walters, solicitors, Streathers, London; Andrew Turvil, Editor of *The Good Food Guide* and the *Which? Pub Guide*; Emma Rickett, The AA; Frances Gill, *Harden's Guides*; Paul Cordle, *The Michelin Guide of Great Britain and Ireland*; Alex Chambers, *Les Routiers Guide*; Soraya Conway, *Zagat Survey*; Sarah Guy, *Time Out Guides*; Georgina Campbell's *Jameson Guide* – Ireland; Julian Shaw, Small Business Service statistics; Joanna Wood, *Caterer and Hotelkeeper*; Simon Henrick, Brake catering; Elizabeth Crompton-Batt, Charles Secrett, Mark Haynes and staunch friends and allies Anna Fleming, Chrissie Bates, Jocelyn and Peter Sampson, Noel Ross-Russell, Caroline Godsmark, Ruth Carver and others who have shown much patience, goodwill encouragement and understanding including Louise, Jackie, Rennie and Gary Reynolds and Guild of Food Writers co-members.

Foreword

Owning and running a restaurant will be, I guarantee, the most exhausting, nerve-wracking and tiring thing you will ever do. If it goes well it will also be the most satisfying and rewarding part of your life - much like raising children. Carol has clearly laid out all the pitfalls you will encounter and the strategies you need to have in place, and if you read this book cover to cover well before you embark on a life as a restaurateur you will be rewarded with foresight. It's a hard life and it can be a great life - but get prepared. Read this book.

Peter Gordon

Dedication

To Jonathan, Matthew and Caroline who lived the restaurant life
to the full

Preface

Are you passionate about restaurants? Do you hanker after opening your own restaurant? You would be entering a very buoyant market as more people are choosing to eat out than ever before. There are over 51,000 restaurants now open for business in Britain, an increase of more than 1,000 in less than a year. This is restaurant boom time.

The rise in people eating out is due, in part, to the structure of households. We are a cash-rich, time-poor society preferring to meet up with friends and family in restaurants rather than slaving over a hot stove at home.

Thanks to an increasing number of wide-ranging types of restaurants offering a greater variety of food to suit every budget, singles, families and older couples in the social demographic mix now eat out on an increasingly regular basis. One in three of us eats out once a week – or more. The customer is now more discerning, able to demand better quality, price, consistency and choice. Otherwise they vote with their feet.

Opening and running a restaurant is an aspiration many people have. They dream of ditching the dull job and entering a world of creativity and hospitality and being their own boss. Or it may naively be seen as a money for old rope venture, tossing a salad or turning a steak under a hot grill being about as vexed as the cooking actually gets. They may also think that customers will be coming through the door on day one without much effort on the new restaurateur's part.

Restaurants are part of the hospitality and entertainment business – it is described as pure theatre – but it is a tough business. It is also a most rewarding, stimulating one, both on a personal level and a financial one if the business is approached and run with prudence, professionalism, control, dedication and a dash of imagination and flair. And you have to like people.

As a restaurant journalist, critic and chef (I am also a restaurant consultant, guide inspector and past restaurateur) I have researched and written

How to Start and Run Your Own Restaurant from an experienced, practical base. The chapters cover aspects of the restaurant trade from location and licence applications to finance and professional advice.

How to Start and Run Your Own Restaurant also covers equipment, marketing, restaurant reviews and staffing to suppliers, menus, wines, the day to day running of the restaurant, complaints and how to deal with them, building up a loyal trade and – crucially – putting yourself in your customers' shoes.

The book is full of up to date information for the novice restaurateur. It also offers advice to those already in the business who may wish to trade up to meet current customer expectations. It includes useful trade addresses, an index and a whole host of top tips throughout the book based on the experiences of seasoned chefs, restaurateurs, suppliers and others in the profession whom I have interviewed for this book.

If your passion for running a restaurant takes hold, I wish you every success and fulfilment in one of the oldest, more rewarding trades in the world, the restaurant and hospitality trade.

1

Running Your Own Restaurant

Becoming a restaurateur either in the UK or taking the plunge abroad is a fantasy many people have. In reality, though, the thought is often put on the back burner due to lack of knowledge on how to proceed, or because the leap from being an employee to becoming self-employed, is daunting.

WHY RUN YOUR OWN RESTAURANT?

As an employee, your work might be unrewarding, unstimulating and pre-dictable, or you may be locked into a profession that no longer inspires. You long to develop a creative and business side you feel you have strengths in and the restaurant world has always attracted you.

Perhaps being in a partnership with family members is appealing, or the urge to control your own destiny is a motivating factor. Could you work with a friend who has agreed to enter into partnership with you?

Being a good cook can be just the catalyst some people need to chuck in the day job and open a restaurant. Their partners hopefully agree to the new venture by also throwing in the corporate towel. But you have to be a very good cook to sustain the business week in week out. Or perhaps you are a good front of house manager/business partner, able to offer excellent hospitality and to manage staff, the accounts, the ordering and the customers.

The good news is that more and more people are eating out. The gratifying result is a mushrooming of restaurants to suit every culinary whim. The bad news is that this business is not suited to all, despite strong aspirations to own and run a restaurant.

HOW SUITABLE ARE YOU?

First examine your strengths and your character – and those in partnership with you – by asking yourself these questions:

- Are you fed up with your job and looking for a change of lifestyle?
- Do you see yourself opening a restaurant in a beautiful spot for an easier lifestyle?
- Do you want to be your own boss and keep the profits?
- Are you really positive about creating a new business?
- Are you motivated, organised and self-disciplined?
- Have you taken on board the fact that you are saying goodbye to a secure pay packet and fringe benefits?
- Have you discussed with your family how this will affect them?
- As your busiest period is weekends, how does this tally with family life?

- Are your family committed to this change of lifestyle and will they back you wholeheartedly?

- Do you like people? Have you skills to deal with the idiosyncrasies of both customers and staff?

- Are you a good communicator?

- Are you prepared for perhaps a long haul before the business is successful?

- Do you and your business partner(s) share the right temperaments for the hospitality business?

- Are you a problem-solver? A decision-maker?

- Are you confident enough to sell your business plan to banks, customers and the media?

- Can you take advice? Learn new skills?

- Can you delegate?

- Can you prioritise?

- How good are you at coping with stress?

- Do you have good health?

- Do you have a warm personality? A hospitable nature?

- Do you have the stamina to work long hours?

- Are you flexible? Calm? Reasonable? Positive?

- How do you really feel about the service industry?

These questions need to be answered honestly. Yes, it is a long list of searching questions. You may have never been tested on some of these strengths but you will need the majority of them to run a successful business. It is worth analysing your personality and those of others who are entering the business with you, both professionally and personally to see if you all have the necessary attributes.

This analytical list is not meant to put you off becoming a restaurateur but merely guide you to become more aware of the skills one needs to aspire to. If many of the answers are in your favour, other attributes will be achieved along the way.

SEEING YOURSELF AS A RESTAURATEUR

Think about what kind of a restaurateur you see yourself as. You might be one who offers acceptable food and is in the business purely as a money-making venture. Or you could be a restaurateur who sees the trade as a way of life. You may seek to change, mature, explore new ideas and learn from other chefs and restaurateurs, but also, through judicious management to, stay afloat financially.

Your restaurant will reflect your personality.

Being a restaurateur *is* a hard, unrelenting, competitive way of life but it can be hugely satisfying, rewarding, pleasurable, entertaining, intense and stimulating. The people you work with are an immensely important factor in making this happen, as well as creating an atmosphere for customers to relax in by offering good food which is thoughtfully and skilfully prepared.

All human life is here. Being a restaurateur requires creativity and passion, boundless energy, commitment and enthusiasm. Dispensing hospitality is either the way of life you choose when running a restaurant – or not. If not, is this the right business for you?

Should you decide to join this way of life, you will be entering one of the oldest professions in the world, one that is very much part of our lives in all cultures. Pure theatre.

2

Choosing Your Restaurant

As the British public, following global trends, are eating out more and more, the types and styles of restaurants have diversified to meet demand. As mentioned in the Preface one in three of us are eating out at least once a week.

DECIDING WHAT KIND OF RESTAURANT

You might want to run a fast food restaurant; a mid-range restaurant; a family-run one. Or perhaps a pasta/pizza eatery; a small restaurant in the town or country; an upmarket one with all the fripperies. Or will you be joining those who take on a pub and create one with good, medium-priced food without all the extras?

Maybe you lean towards a restaurant serving ethnic food; a daytime opening café or tea room serving freshly made lunches and teas; a mainly fish restaurant or an informal one offering all manner of inexpensive food for the passing tourist trade.

As the restaurant trade is so diverse, you will have to do a lot of research before settling on an area. Is there a glut of pizza/pasta restaurants already in the neighbourhood? As this is chain territory, there is already a plethora of these types. Or do you think you can offer even better pizza and pasta than those already on offer and price them competitively? Think of their buying power, advertising, big business backing and think again.

As I've mentioned, independent gastro pubs are taking on the restaurant trade both in town and country, customers flocking to them in their droves. It started in 1990, when London's The Eagle in Clerkenwell re-invented the traditional pub by offering mainly modern, British, gutsy, unfussy food. Top ingredients are used with a minimum of chefs in an unforced, unpretentious atmosphere. It is unfancy, simple, yet effective, and memorable if in the right hands.

Repeat business is guaranteed if you've got the right feel and the right food, a good selection of wines by the glass and bottle and decent on-tap local beers. And, it goes without saying, good, knowledgeable, friendly staff.

Will you welcome children into your restaurant? In Britain children are largely seen as a bit of a nuisance, unlike our European cousins who tend to welcome children into their restautants with open arms. In France and other countries, a family with children isn't shunted into a special area as is the norm in Britain, especially in chain restaurants. Instead, they are genuinely welcomed and given an ordinary table anywhere in the restaurant, not just in the back recesses.

Children are treated like customers (as they should be!) and eat the food their parents eat. They are not fobbed off with chicken nuggets and chips. As a result, these children grow up with a more rounded understanding of food and how to behave in a social setting, as their parents actually talk to them rather than just reprimand them. It is surely time to create the same principles for our children and not ban them from restaurants.

As Matthew Fort, food journalist for the *Guardian Weekend* and past restaurant reviewer noted on a visit to a hotel restaurant: 'It's hotel policy to ban children under the age of 12, a policy that I overhead being enthusiastically endorsed by a party at a nearby table. It sent me into a towering rage. How typically middle-aged, middle-class, blinkered, selfish and British. I can think of no justification for marginalising children in this way, particularly as, in my experience, they can often give their elders a lesson in manners.'

I totally agree. To paraphase John Lennon, give children a chance.

NEW TRENDS IN RESTAURANTS

New, good restaurants are cropping up in surprising parts of the UK. What is lacking are good neighbourhood restaurants for everyday eating as found in many other countries.

Delicatessens with restaurants

Delicatessens with attached restaurants are also on the increase and can either open all day and evening or, depending on their location, only during the day to catch the city's business trade. They have cropped up in London, Bristol, Brighton, Chichester, Manchester and Totnes and in other towns in Devon to great acclaim.

All-day cafés

Other trends include all-day cafés serving excellent breakfasts, elevenses (where else in the world except Britain?), brunches, light lunches and teas. They may also open in the evening as a more upmarket restaurant and maximise the potential of the space to cover the high costs of maintaining the site.

Following the trends

These new trends may be a good route to take. Take into consideration where you are based. Is there a passing trade? You could offer good loose-leaf tea, the best coffee and a good range of simple, easily-prepared dishes for those in a hurry. Consider whether you appeal to the shopper, or those on business in the area.

The New Zealand chef, Peter Gordon, well known for his fusion food, is a prime example of how to do this with style, wit, verve and simplicity. The Providores, the award-winning London restaurant he jointly owns with three partners, is a union of restaurant, all-day café, meeting place and wine bar.

The casual, professionally run place offers the lot – laksas, tortillas, soups, freshly baked breads, bowls of nuts and olives, sardines, soy braised duck, New Zealand venison, smoothies, teas, coffees, freshly squeezed juices *et al* – in the downstairs Tapa Room from 9 am to 10.30 pm. The Providores upstairs offers an equally eclectic fusion mix of dishes on its constantly changing menu.

Beyond the cities

Can this mix be achieved outside large cities?

West Sussex's Chichester has a similar (bar the breakfasts) restaurant. The Dining Room is a wine bar cum restaurant offering not only tapas but also Danish open sandwiches. Included on the menu are charcuterie and specially selected cheese plates, salads, starters, game, beef, lamb and fish main courses and omelettes. In short, the owners made a decision to appeal to a broad market including pre-theatre diners. And it works because it has researched its market and has responded to it.

Small, family-run restaurants with minimal seating and offering terrific, authentic Middle-Eastern food are proving to be immensely popular too. Prices are low, and the atmosphere, created by hookahs, low sofas and Arab music, make these restaurants popular places to eat. So far, these are springing up in east London to great acclaim, and the trend will no doubt follow to cities with an urban mix of nationalities.

3

Location, Design and Legal Requirements

Having narrowed down the area where you wish to run your business you must then decide whether to buy or rent a property. First you'll need to contact commercial property estate agents who will offer you their considerable wealth of local knowledge. For example:

◆ What are the trends in the restaurant trade?

◆ Will you need planning permission?

◆ How do you negotiate the property ladder?

You will also need to talk to environmental health officers about required standards for running a restaurant.

This chapter deals with these subjects and also provides tips for scrutinising properties, buying, renting, franchising and leases. It also deals with:

◆ local government issues;

◆ refuse collection;

◆ alcohol and public entertainment licenses;

◆ fire regulations;

◆ disabled law;

◆ the Sale of Goods Act;

◆ the law concerning Sex Discrimination and Race Relations Act;

◆ the Hotel Proprietor's Act;

◆ water supply and pest control advice;

◆ kitchen layout;

◆ ventilation;

◆ the vexed question of music and smoking;

◆ and a final check list.

LOCATION, LOCATION, LOCATION

The popular conception for a truly successful restaurant is that the three Ls are sacrosant. In a city this is true as customers are close by, whether they live, work or are staying in hotels near to your restaurant.

By contrast, some of the most successful restaurants are in remote areas. So how do they create a good, solid customer base? Thanks to the superb ingredients cooked to a high standard and the sheer beauty of the location, people will make the detour to a well-run, perhaps seasonal, restaurant.

Compare the restaurant Gordon Ramsay in London's Chelsea where you need to book months in advance and the highly popular The Three Chimneys on the Isle of Skye, a 40-seater restaurant down a single track. One is about as remote as it gets on the British Isles, the other by contrast one of the most central.

Whatever the location, what really matters is how the business is run once the right location has been chosen.

Narrowing it down

You've decided on your area and are thinking of buying or renting a property. Visit it a number of times on different days and times of the day. This will give you a better flavour of the area, the type of people, the activity, and will also give you a more informed view of the property. Does the lighting need improving, the decoration updating, the entrance made more welcoming and accessible?

If possible, sit for a time in the restaurants you have narrowed down and imagine a business working in the building. Does it suit your plans? Is it enhanced by a view, a character? Are the proportions right?

Outline your plans to friends or those in the restaurant business and talk over the space with them. They may be able to throw light on a particular problem that has so far eluded you. Or they may give good advice as to why not to open such a place in the area.

Put yourself in your customers' shoes. If competitors are based in the same area, are there too many of the same type of restaurant as yours? You may struggle for business unless you offer something quite different. But, equally, you may pick up overflow from successful nearby restaurants if the public see the area as a place for eating out.

There is usually a good reason for a gastronomic desert. Look at Guildford in Surrey. Very few good restaurants and nothing worth a mention in the *Good Food Guide*. Why? Easy commuting into London where many commuting residents prefer eating out is one explanation. Expensive property is another.

SPOTTING CURRENT TRENDS

Consumer education about food continues to increase thanks to travel abroad. The emphasis on food, drink, produce and hospitality in the media is also continuing at an unprecedented pace. So the question you might ask is 'why can't I get that here?'

Expectations are constantly rising. There are many price levels to choose from as well as styles of cooking, restaurant design and atmosphere. Who would have thought basement premises could be sold as desirable places to eat in? Step up Wagamama, the runaway successful slurping noodle chain which established their restaurants in basements. Their style of fast, casual and good food is a runaway hit. But a word of warning: few other basement restaurants do achieve this. Or upstairs restaurants. People like to see the whole place at street level.

Some current trends to look out for:

◆ High inner city rents, thanks to corporate businesses vying for hot property spots and willing to pay over the odds, have meant that restaurateurs are now looking at suburbs, smaller towns and the countryside for properties.

◆ Individual neighbourhood restaurants are making a comeback thanks to the public's disaffection with branded restaurants and pubs as they are looking for a more personal approach.

◆ Due to drink-drive regulations and difficulties with parking, neighbourhood restaurants have the edge over their drive-to competitors.

◆ Conveyor belt ethnic food – Japanese, Chinese, Thai, Indian – is also gaining favour with younger eaters.

◆ Gastro pubs have been increasingly popular in London for at least 14 years and are making their mark in the rest of the UK and Ireland. There is more profit in quality food than in drink.

◆ Run-down pubs are popular premises to buy and turn into wine bars or cafés with the emphasis on bistro-type food.

- There is a big resurgence in developing inner city areas and dock areas such as Bristol, Liverpool and Newcastle with restaurants opening up to fill demand.

- Small, simple, very casual, minimal comfort combined deli-cafés are opening in cities to attract the business crowd during office hours and early evening.

- Small niche restaurants are opening in medium-sized and large towns.

- Fast/casual restaurants are in great demand not only by customers but by venture capital investors.

- Contemporarily designed restaurants with clean lines, wooden floorboards, good lighting and music attract customers and will continue to do so, say agents. Carpeted premises, and not being able to see inside premises from the street, are big turnoffs.

- The first 24-hour cafés are to open once deregulation of licensing laws takes place.

- One in three Londoners eat out at least once a week. The rest of Britain is slower to react but this is set to change thanks to trends in working/leisure patterns and an older population who can afford to eat out.

FIRST STEPS TO TAKE ON THE PROPERTY LADDER

First get yourself a solicitor who specialises in commercial property transactions for either renting or buying a property. Draw up a business plan and then get it approved by your bank.

If you are renting, prepare a good presentation pack to win the landlord's approval. Use some graphics to inject that wow factor, particularly if the property is in London as that is expected in the capital. Out of town presentation doesn't need to be as sophisticated, according to commercial property agents.

Do put in the presentation: the anticipated covers, the spend per head, if you intend to turn tables (i.e. the same table to be used several times at one sitting) and the proposed accounting.

Go through the *Yellow Pages* or buy a catering magazine such as *Caterer and Hotelkeeper* to see who the agents are in your area. Good agents will get to know you, the client, instead of a scattergun approach of introducing you to masses of properties that don't suit your wishes. Be sure you make it clear to the agent what kind of property you are seeking. But be prepared to be flexible when viewing properties as you may surprise yourself.

First and foremost, however, there must be an excellent understanding of your market. This comes first before entering into any contract, despite the excitement of falling in love with a property. Do you fit into this area? Who will your customers be?

Renting the property

If renting a restaurant premises, measure the property yourself. The area given by estate agents or landlords could be less and the rent should therefore to be lowered. Negotiate a lower rent if taking out a long lease.

If the property needs repairs or major redecoration, ask for a rent-free period or discount until these are carried out.

Always get an agreement in writing for all dealings with landlords or estate agents, especially for any major alterations you would like to make to the property. Check on planning permission with your local council if putting up new signage or change of use of a property.

Buying leasehold or freehold

Find an architect whose practice deals in restaurant development. Get them to visit the property with you to discuss any alterations you may like to make and be guided by his or her expertise.

Check on planning permission with the your local council re change of use, signage and access to property via new doors, for example. Instruct a solicitor to act for you.

◆ **TOP TIP** ◆

Communication is vital between buyer and seller. Keep people up to speed.

Discuss with environmental health officers basic requirements such as hand basins for staff, refrigeration, kitchen extractors, fire extinguishers (see page 66 for a fuller view of the EHO's role and expectations).

Questions to ask

Before buying or renting an established restaurant ask:

◆ Is the area saturated with similar restaurants?

◆ Are the owners experiencing restaurant burnout or are there other reasons for the sale/change of lease?

◆ Is there local development which will adversely affect the area? Or, conversely, add to the customer potential?

◆ How old is the business and for how many years has it been profitable?

◆ What is the profit margin for the past few years?

◆ What percentage of repeat business is there?

◆ Do the books look accurate? Do the assets outweigh the liabilities?

◆ Ask your solicitor's or bank manager's advice.

◆ Have all renovations been undertaken with the necessary approval?

Leases: a brief guide

The average leasehold lease is 25 years with other leases at 20 or 15 years, but other leases can be negotiated with the landlord. A freehold lease's finance changes only with the cost of borrowing.

◆ Landlords are looking for long-term investments and if the tenant has no track record, the landlord may ask for a rent deposit of a year in advance or a bank guarantee.

◆ However, the tenant may ask for a rent-free period if money is being spent on the property such as for rewiring, redecorating, new plumbing.

◆ The lease should be a full repairing and insuring one with five year rent reviews, the rent only increasing, never decreasing.

◆ The amount of rent increase can be calculated on profits or a comparable method of calculation.

◆ A break clause is advisable. This is a walk-away sum should the lease be broken.

◆ A sub-let clause should also be included.

◆ It is of course advisable to get professional advice with a lease.

◆ The shorter the lease, the less security there is for the restaurant and its borrowing power.

◆ A longer lease could be used as security against a loan as well as give a psychological feeling of security.

◆ Ask a tax advisor about setting off a large rent deposit against taxes as the period of non-profit making needs to be taken into account.

◆ Get the rent right as this is key to a successful restaurant.

The property and timing from viewing to signing a contract

From viewing to signing via legalities and licensing your property can vary from eight to 12 weeks depending on the complexities of the property and the availability of your finances. It can also be affected by your council's efficiency.

If the restaurant is a shell and needs planning permission and licensing it may take three to five months. Change of use can take one month.

◆ Good communication is vital with all parties involved.

FRANCHISING A BUSINESS

The market for franchising a restaurant business is still within the fast food arena with the likes of Domino's Pizza, Dunking Donuts and Baskin

Robbins to choose from. Mid-market franchising has been considered by better quality companies but little has appeared to date. Franchising can apply to any type of restaurant.

The concept behind franchising is taking a proven format and, to replicate it, a franchisee invests in the setting up of the premises (McDonalds set-ups can be up to £250,000 to kit out one of their outlets) and shares the profits.

It is a very safe way of opening a restaurant if the spirit of being an entrepreneur doesn't appeal. Customers come from day one as they know and like the product. Kentucky Fried Chicken is a case in point versus Bert's Fried Chicken. Ninety-five per cent of franchises are profitable in year five.

But it is not for the work-shy. It takes extremely hard work, the franchisee is regularly checked and the rules of operation are very strict.

The trend towards franchising has slowed down quite dramatically, however, thanks to good employment during a stable economic cycle.

LOCAL GOVERNMENT AND YOUR BUSINESS

You need to establish a relationship with your local authority for planning permission, building regulations and any structural changes you wish to make to the property. Are you converting a property? Custom-building one? It is vital to get their advice and/or permission before embarking on any building.

- Get approval for change of use permission if converting a property.

- Consider consulting a professional to sort out the paperwork if the process is complicated – and for your sanity.

- If you wish to lodge a complaint against your local authority if you feel the handling of your application was badly undertaken, contact the authority first, then a higher authority if still dissatisfied. You may wish to discuss the possible steps with your solicitor or a professional planning consultant.

SCRUTINISING THE EXTERIOR AND INTERIOR OF A PROPERTY

View properties with a fine-tooth comb attitude. To help you to negotiate your price have a sound checklist and a list of items to discuss with builders for quotations:

◆ Are there cracks or any visible structural problems?

◆ Are the ceilings flaking? Any damp patches?

◆ Is the flooring, particularly in the kitchen areas, suitable and in good condition?

◆ Is there good drainage?

◆ Does the flooring slope, or have holes, is it uneven, are there changes of floor level?

◆ Are kitchen surfaces and equipment surfaces in sound condition?

◆ Is there adequate lighting or does new lighting have to be installed?

◆ Do stairs have hand rails?

◆ Are windows in good order? Check for rotting wood.

◆ Is the roof sound?

◆ Does the whole property need to be redecorated?

◆ Is there good ventilation?

◆ Is there an adequate supply of hot water and drinking water?

◆ Is appropriate fire safety installed?

◆ If equipment such as fridges and cookers are included in the deal, are they moveable to clean behind, in good working order, well maintained and clean?

KITCHEN LAYOUT

To provide a safe working environment, and to avoid cross contamination of food at all stages, the design of your kitchen and service areas is of great importance. Your layout should be built around the operation and not the other way around. Points to consider include:

◆ The same basic rules apply irrespective of size or scale of the establishment.

◆ An older building such as a seventeenth century cottage with a restaurant may not have the perfect layout. Take this into consideration when looking at properties and decide if the areas can be made to work – or not. Can staff in the working area carry work out safely?

◆ A logical flow of operation of delivery, storage, prepping, cooking, serving, disposal of waste, rubbish storage and collection with as many clearly designated areas for each stage of work is necessary to avoid cross contamination.

For example, a box is delivered and is put down on the counter where chicken is being prepared. Not only can the box have dirt on the bottom but it may now have picked up raw chicken bits. That box may be moved to another part of the kitchen and the cross contamination is now in its second stage.

The kitchen counter may also be contaminated from dirt on the box, the box perhaps having been put down on the pavement prior to being taken into the restaurant. All of this can be avoided if a logical flow – and common sense – is adhered to.

◆ Is space limited so that efficiency is impaired?

◆ Is cleaning difficult?

◆ Is there sufficient space for people to work at benches (counters to you and me) and other fixed equipment to allow other people to pass?

◆ The layout of cookers, ovens, fryers, refrigeration and other hot machinery with or without moving parts must be taken into account to avoid congestion.

Ventilation requirements

Good ventilation provides a comfortable working environment, reduces humidity, removes contaminated greasy air, steam and cooking smells. It also prevents condensation and will ultimately help on redecoration and maintenance.

Cost-cutting can result in high temperatures and humidity with increased risk of food poisoning. Good maintenance is essential to remain effective. External ducts require planning permission in most cases and need to be positioned carefully to avoid fallout with neighbours.

There are three main types of ventilation:

1. Natural ventilation: only suitable for small-scale operations, this system is seldom ideal as it relies on open windows and doors, is subject to weather whims and is least effective in hot weather. Mesh screening is necessary to keep out flying insects.

2. Extract only system: a simple, inexpensive technique which uses an extractor fan to draw out hot or stale air, cooking fumes and steam. Useful to ensure that cooking smells are prevented from spreading to other rooms.

3. Combined extract/inlet system: the most efficient system with the fullest control, it balances the flow of air in and out of the area. The design is based on a combination of ducting and fan exhausting the hot, damp and sometimes greasy air from the area with controllable replacement fresh air.

Hygiene facilities

Adequate water supply, wash basins, sinks, washing up equipment and good draining are of paramount importance in setting up your restaurant.

Water supply and drainage

Drinkable (also known as potable) water must be used to ensure food is not contaminated. In addition:

♦ Only drinkable water can be used to make ice cubes.

♦ Water from a storage tank or private water supply has to be monitored on a regular basis.

♦ In new premises, drinking water installation should be disinfected. Your local authority or architect can advise.

- Drainage facilities must be designed and constructed to avoid the risk of contamination of foodstuffs.

- All sink, wash basin and dishwasher pipes should discharge directly into the drainage system through a trapped gully to prevent foul odours.

- As this is a complex area with floor channels, deep seal gullies and sewers, do contact your local authority for further information.

Sinks and washing up equipment

Adequate facilities for food preparation, staff use, crockery, general cleaning and disinfecting of work tools and equipment all require a supply of hot and cold water, and must be easily cleanable and well sited.

- Lavatories must not be next to food handling space.

- Hand washing facilities must be provided in prep areas with hot and cold water and materials for cleaning hands.

- Sinks for washing food must be separate from hand washing sinks.

- Separate hand wash basins are recommended to be placed in each work and food service area including the bar, and preferably at the entrance of the kitchen.

- Stainless steel wash basins are strongly recommended but glazed ceramic basins are acceptable. Domestic sinks are not acceptable.

- Wash basins with foot, knee, 'automatic operated' taps or mixer taps are deemed a good idea but are not necessary.

- Position hand dryers carefully so that dirt and bacteria aren't blown around food areas. As they are slow and inefficient, perhaps putting off frequent hand washing, disposable towels are your best bet.

- One or more commercial quality stainless steel sinks are recommended for the main sinks with one or more deep sinks for pot washing.

- In large catering premises separate sinks are required for each of the following: vegetables, salads, meat and fish.

◆ A dishwashing machine with a fitted water softener (for certain hard water areas) is recommended for all but the smallest of food premises. Commercial dishwashers take very little time in comparison to domestic dishwashers to operate and are designed with a simple interior and simple controls.

◆ A double sink with double stainless steel (never wooden) drainer is also recommended and may be used instead of a dishwasher but why be hard on yourself?

◆ The bar might have a glass washing machine and/or a sink (single/double) with double drainer.

◆ A separate sink for mops, buckets etc should be located outside the food area.

These are recommendations only. Take advice from your Environmental Health officer, particularly if you have small premises with little space.

Refuse storage

Even smart restaurants like Rick Stein's Seafood Restaurant in Padstow have difficulties with rubbish due to lack of space outside. If you do have the space do position free standing bins well away from the view of diners as this can be very off-putting. Some restaurants don't follow this aesthetically pleasing advice. If you want repeat business place bins strategically if possible.

◆ Don't allow food waste and other refuse to accumulate in food rooms.

◆ Waste must be in closed, sound, easy to clean containers.

◆ Free-standing or wall mounted lidded holders for plastic bags should be provided, or a foot operated plastic lidded bin lined with a plastic bag.

◆ Remove full bags, and clean containers and surrounding area frequently.

◆ Refuse storage and removal must be arranged and designed to be protected from pests (those pesky flying insects, cats, dogs and foxes in particular) and mustn't contaminate premises, drinking water or equipment.

◆ Either site refuse storage externally with a roofed shield if space allows or in a non-food area with plenty of ventilation.

◆ Keep wheeliebins clean and clearly marked with the restaurant name.

◆ For larger businesses bulk collection of refuse can be arranged. One large London restaurant mixes up its refuse collection and uses 120 local authority paid bags a week at a cost of over £1,500 a year. Pigswill bins, bottles and boxes are collected by another firm. The pigswill is 'cooked' in vats by steam and fed to pigs.

◆ Contact your local authority for what is on offer as the type of service offered varies as well as charges. Contact them too for disposal of white goods (fridges and freezers for example).

Pest control

Keeping those infestations of rodents, insects or other food pests out is a priority:

◆ Any infestation will lead to contamination of food and food surfaces, damage of food stocks and the building.

◆ To combat this, the maintenance of high standards of cleanliness, good housekeeping, food storage and proofing of the building should be undertaken.

◆ Both country and town have vermin problems with cockroaches, mice, pharaoh ants (tiny brown ants) and rats, all of which can be dealt with by local authority or private contractor exterminators.

◆ The cleaner your restaurant, and that means behind fridges etc where vermin love to congregate, the less problems you'll encounter.

◆ TOP TIP ◆

Gloss paint encourages condensation. Artex ceilings are not accepted due to difficulty with cleaning, and polystyrene or acoustic tiles are unlikely to be passed. Ceiling tiles should be fire retardant.

FIRST IMPRESSIONS

First impressions of your restaurant are vital.

- Is it welcoming and well kept?

- Is it well lit?

- Is there any cracked paint?

- Are the windows clean, the entrance swept and door handles polished?

- Are the menu and times of opening visible?

- Is the entrance to the car park clearly signed?

- If you have a garden and paths are they well maintained?

If these are ignored, customers will ignore you and go elsewhere. If the property looks dirty, they'll wonder what the kitchens and toilets are like.

All properties need the basics over and above the obvious such as a dining area, kitchen and loos: office space for paperwork, good storage space other than the kitchen for supplies including wine, rubbish (where to store it until collection), staff lockers or storage area for personal belongings.

◆ TOP TIP ◆

Keep your entrance clutter-free for easy access for able-bodied and disabled customers alike.

LICENCES

Alcohol licences

Under the Licensing Bill 2003, significant changes were made by the government including that it is councils, not the magistrates' court, who now deal with licences.

A premises licence will be required by pubs, restaurants, businesses offering hot food between 11 pm and 5 am, hotels, guest houses and other places that sell alcohol.

A **personal licence** will be needed by anyone who allows the sale of alcohol and is valid for ten years. There are various duties on holders of personal licences and the court can cancel your licence if you are convicted of certain offences.

To get a personal licence you must be over 18, not have any relevant criminal convictions as spelt out in the Act, possess an approved licensing qualification and pay the required fee.

The four licensing objectives are:

1. Prevention of crime and disorder.

2. Prevention of public nuisance.

3. Public safety.

4. Prevention of harm to children.

Premises licences

A premise licence can be granted either for a one-off event or indefinitely. Applicants have to submit a plan of their building, an operating schedule (a brief description of how the premises will be operated safely) and a fee, expected to be in the region of £500 maximum. Contact your local authority to find out the cost.

Temporary and occasional events

Licences will not be needed for small events where less than 500 people are likely to attend, and the event lasts for less than 72 hours.

Someone with a personal licence will be able to hold up to 50 temporary or occasional events a year at other premises that are not licensed. Non-personal licence holders will be able to hold up to five temporary events a year.

A **Temporary Event Notice** must be given to the Council before an event of this sort can be held and the police may object to it on crime and disorder grounds.

Contact your district council for guidance on how to obtain a licence and your local trading standards officer for alcohol measurement guidelines.

Public Entertainment Licences

If music, entertainment or dancing are to be held, a Public Entertainment Licence may be required. Contact your Environmental Health Officer who will also give advice on prevention of noise nuisance.

Notification of Accidents

Employers must contact the Environmental Health Office about any fatality, major injury, accident or dangerous occurrence that happens on their premises, under the Reporting of Injuries, Diseases and Occurences Regulations 1995.

Fire Certification

Some types of food businesses require a Fire Certificate. Consult your local Fire Prevention Officer.

MUSIC

As a restaurant critic I receive letters on many aspects of restaurants from disgruntled customers, with music high up on their list of pet hates. Often the music is played, seemingly, for the benefit of the staff: very loud and inappropriate. When I do suggest it might be turned down, I am often looked at with contempt. The message is that I am interrupting *their* party.

Music can of course enhance the atmosphere of a restaurant, putting people in the mood for a good time as soon as they enter the door. Conversely, it can alienate customers. If they need to shout to have a conversation, clearly this is unacceptable.

If your restaurant's atmosphere creates hushed tones you may wish to inject some suitable music, but do listen to your customers. Often silence, that rare commodity, is golden. And appreciated in our increasingly noisy society.

If you play recorded music in the restaurant you will need to have a licence from the Performing Rights Society. The tariff applies to performances in the UK of copyright music within the Society's repertoire at hotels, restaurants, cafés, fast food outlets, banqueting suites, function rooms, boarding houses and guesthouses. Currently, only theatre restaurants, theatre cafés and similar premises are exempt.

Email: musiclicence@prs.co.uk, contact www.prs.co.uk or call (0800) 068 48 28 for advice.

For live music see Licenses above.

SMOKING

There is currently (2004) no legislation banning smoking in restaurants, pubs, cafés and similar establishments as in Ireland, but do keep an eye open for this legislation which is a hot topic in government circles.

Most restaurants operate a smoking and a no smoking area with a ban on cigars and pipes. Others have an outright ban and some allow smoking after a certain time. Some restaurateurs add a notice on the menu for customers to respect others dining near to them in the vague hope that a civil attitude will come to the fore.

There are good air extraction systems available which may remove those noxious fumes that literally get up the noses of non-smokers. The debate is a heated one, with many customers opposed to any smoking on premises. Increasing numbers of customers enquire about smoking before booking and will not book if smoking is allowed. And vice versa.

Staff smoking is a real problem too as they congregate (usually) outside the kitchen door in view of passing trade. This is unacceptable as it gives the wrong impression. Smoking plays real havoc with getting the most out of food and wine as it dulls the palate. If your chefs smoke what does this say about their tasting ability?

Non-smoking staff are passive smokers, a health risk when taking on a restaurant job. Could legislation follow as this is a human rights issue?

COMPLYING WITH ACTS

Disabled access and facilities

Do consult the planning department regarding disabled access, space within the restaurant and toilets designed for wheelchair access. An existing restaurant in an eighteenth century building, for example, may not need to have a ramp but any new builds have to conform to disability laws.

Amendments to The Disability Discrimination Act 1995 which came into force in October 2004 require you to address any physical features which make it difficult to use your restaurant. These include:

◆ steps, stairways, kerbs;

◆ parking, exterior surfaces and paving;

◆ building entrances and signage;

◆ toilet and washing facilities;

◆ public facilities;

◆ lifts and escalators.

In some cases it may be unreasonable through cost or planning legislation to make these changes. Contact your local authority or the Papworth Trust: www.papworth.org.uk to find out about requirements, guide dogs for the blind and other issues that affect disabled people. For further information log on to www.disability.gov.uk

There are eight-and-a-half million disabled people in the UK, with one in four customers being disabled or close to someone who is. The following are recommended:

- Think and plan ahead to meet the requirements of your disabled customers.

- Don't make assumptions about disabled people based on speculation and stereotypes.

- Communicate a positive policy to providing services to disabled customers and staff.

Sale of Goods and Trades Description

As a trader you must be aware of the Sale of Goods Act which implies that there is an unexpressed contract when you accept a customer's order. The customer may either demand a replacement by right or refuse to pay. Some examples:

- If the goods don't correspond with the description, eg, roast chicken which has been poached instead of being grilled.

- If artificial cream is offered instead of fresh cream.

- If the food is inedible.

Even if the customer has partly or wholly consumed the food it makes no difference. The Trades Description Act makes it a criminal offence to misdescribe goods or services. Watch out for the following:

- wording on menus and wine lists;

- describing food and drink to customers verbally;

- describing services, eg. cover and service charges or extras;

- describing services on offer.

The defence, if someone is charged under the Act, is to prove that reasonable precautions were taken and:

- the result of pure mistake;

- the result of information from someone else;

◆ the fault of someone else;

◆ the result of accident or other cause beyond the control of the person concerned;

◆ the person charged could not reasonably know the description was misleading.

For Trading Standards alcohol requirements see Chapter 10 (wine and other drinks).

Discrimination

The Sex Discrimination Act and the Race Relations Act both legislate against discrimination on grounds of colour, race, creed or sex.

◆ Refusing service to customers of particular colour, race, creed or sex.

◆ Refusing services by imposing unjustifiable conditions or requirements for these same groups of people.

◆ Victimisation via refusal of entry, providing a poor service to ethnic customers which is inferior to those offered to the general public, or which may only be available at a price premium.

The Hotel Proprietors Act

The hotel premises' management is under no obligation to serve anyone unless customers are staying in a hotel or similar establishment. Reasons for refusal could be:

◆ There is no space left.

◆ The person is drunk.

◆ The person is under the influence of drugs.

◆ The customer is not suitably dressed.

◆ The person is a known trouble-maker.

◆ The person is an associate of a known trouble-maker.

- The person is under the legal minimum age for licensed premises or does not fit into the age policy set by the premises.

- Under the Licensed Premises (Exclusion of Certain Persons) Act 1980 the licensee has the right to refuse entry to people who are drunk, violent and disorderly, quarrelsome or appear unable to pay.

- It is an offence to sell intoxicating liquor to a drunk person or those under 18 years of age.

PRICE MARKING (FOOD AND DRINK ON PREMISES) ORDER 1979

Prices of food and drink must be displayed in a clear and legible way by persons selling food by retail for consumption on the premises, but this does not apply to members of a club or their guests, in staff restaurants or in guest houses, however communicative and civilised that would be. Private catering menus are also excluded but the following provisions must be taken into account.

Menu and a drinks list must be at the entrance or be able to be read from the street. If part of a complex, the list must be shown at the entrance to the eating area. Both food and drink must be included. Table d'hôte (set menu) prices must be given. VAT must be included and a service and/or a cover charge must be shown as an amount or a percentage.

In self-service premises where the customer chooses food, prices must be shown at the entrance unless they can be seen at the counter.

YOUR CHECKLIST

Ask yourself:

- Have you registered your premises?

- Do the design and construction of your premises meet legal requirements?

- Have you considered all the health and fire safety requirements?

- Do you and your staff understand the principles of good food hygiene?

- Have you and your staff had food hygiene training?

- Have you considered what food safety problems there could be at each stage of the business?

- Have you put the necessary food safety procedures in place and are you making regular checks to ensure they are working?

- Do you describe food and drink accurately?

- Do you need to apply for a licence to sell alcohol?

- Have you registered as self-employed?

- Do you need to register for VAT?

- Are you keeping records of all your business income and expenses?

- Are you keeping records of your employees' pay and do you know how to pay their tax and National Insurance contributions?

4

Financing Your Business

As Kit Chapman, restaurateur/owner of The Castle Hotel, Taunton, Somerset and of the Brazz brasseries, and countless others in the business says, 'making money is the first priority.'

Other reasons for opening a restaurant come into the equation. They include creating a restaurant to suit your personality, offering hospitality and being in a trade rather more interesting than the average thanks to its high profile, sexy image. Is opening a restaurant a romantic ideal or a profitable business proposal? Can the two meet?

CREATING INCOME

The advice of successful restaurateurs is to never lose sight of your livelihood – and that of your partners, family and staff. Wise words. It is so seductive being your own boss in this entertainment/food world that it is quite easy to lose the prime plot: your income.

Curb your naturally generous instincts with friends when they visit your restaurant. It is all very well offering wine on the house, a meal, coffees. They may come to expect it, such is human nature. Instead, become shrewd and be aware of margins and curb your bountiful nature.

Take a leaf out of corporate industries' practice and have a loss leader on the menu. Shop around for good, quality produce and equipment rather than succumbing at the first shopping expedition to the jauntiest fridge with all the bells and whistles. Negotiate. Haggle. It still does happen in the western world. Be armed with good information, prices, and an understanding of the market when dealing with any part of the restaurant's finances.

In the honeymoon period the curiosity value of a new restaurant brings in diners. Once this is over the finance part of the business may need to be revised, and long-term strategies with stages of development built in to the picture.

Steps to developing a financial base

Some restaurants don't lose that honeymoon period but create enough interest to attract a growing band of loyal and new customers. They continue to develop a working financial base and have put into practice the art of producing consistent quality food, good service, conviviality, atmosphere and value for money. Constantly analysing, updating and re-inventing your business is as important as never losing sight of the art of hospitality.

This finance chapter deals with:

◆ raising capital;

◆ creating a business plan;

◆ forming a company;

- planning overheads;

- trading projections;

- financial records;

- and tips.

It deals with issues like raising capital, business partner advice, capital expenditure and steps in funding. Accountancy and getting to grips with good book-keeping practice, legalities, insurance and VAT are other essentials for sound finance.

The chapter also discusses service charges, menu supplement charges and what these extras, hidden or not, say about your business.

Help with the national minimum age payments, pensions and other staff issues are in Chapter 8.

A BUSINESS PLAN

First, you need to work out your initial proposal of the type of restaurant you wish to run. For example:

- Its name, location, concept.

- Who your customers will be.

- What is on your menu and your drink list.

- Your staffing and purchase costings, rental and projected income per day.

Business plans are recommended by most experts, the banks in particular demanding them for further discussion. However, many entrepreneurs operate without them. But if you are not 100% sure that your restaurant plan will work without one, then think of a business plan as being an asset, your strength.

These plans are, of course, not a guarantee for success but by identifying the strengths and weaknesses of your idea, you will greatly improve your chances of succeeding. The plan, however, needs updating as it is a working tool. It's your map to success. But there comes a time to stop planning and to put your goals into action.

To build on the initial proposal follow these steps:

- **Executive summary**: describe the business in general terms in approximately one page.

- **Overview**: your mission. What are you looking to achieve? Why do you think it will work?

- **Introduction**: your restaurant's purpose, your expertise and history and those of your partners, your staff (should you have a chef lined up, for example), and your critical success factors (what is going to make it work).

- **Business environment**: your market research into your type of restaurant, its potential re location, problems and possible solutions, the competition and an expansion potential (running outside catering, for example).

- **Make your presentation professional-looking**. A messy jumble of ideas randomly put on paper will not improve anyone's chances of getting to the next stage of discussions. Instead, choose a business-like font, put ideas under headings, check the spelling and present it in a titled folder with perhaps some clear drawings. Make several copies to hand out.

FORMING A COMPANY

If you decide to operate as a company, you will have to pay corporation tax and make company tax returns. The corporation tax self assessment from the Inland Revenue deals with this. Soon after the end of the accounting period they will send you a notice asking you to make a company tax return.

You must normally pay any tax due by nine months and one day after the end of the accounting period. If you have not yet completed your company tax return you must make an estimate of what you think is due and pay that.

Send a completed tax return, including your accounts and tax computations, to the Inland Revenue by the filing date which is usually 12 months after the end of the accounting period. If the return is not delivered by this date, a penalty will occur.

Maintain proper business records and keep these for six years after the end of the accounting period.

Speak to your accountant or tax advisor to decide on the accounting period and tell your tax office. Work out the dates by which you need to pay tax and make your company tax return.

Plan ahead to make sure that accounts and tax computations are prepared in good time for this, but always communicate with your tax office if you fall behind. Make sure it's a two-way dialogue for peace of mind.

CALCULATING MENU COSTINGS AND PRICES

Getting menu pricing wrong has been the downfall of many a new restaurant and, as a general rule of thumb, successful restaurants work on a 65 per cent gross profit (GP), excluding VAT. Once you have calculated the costs of any dish, multiply them by 3.3. You can't go too far wrong but, of course, there are exceptions to the 65 per cent gross profit rule.

To calculate your gross profit margin, it is first necessary to work out the cost of each dish on the menu. But first, get price lists from wholesale companies and other suppliers including pricing goods at retail shops, farm shops, specialist mail order food companies and other sources such as van drivers delivering produce in the area.

If you are going to specialise in fresh fish, for example, are there any good suppliers in the area or do you need to source quality fish from further away? Ask for advice from a friendly, trustworthy restaurateur who they use, look up fish suppliers in the *Yellow Pages* in your area and further afield like London and Brixham.

Working out the costs

Calculate everything that goes into that particular recipe including the garnishes if using any, the butter the fish might be cooked in, the VAT and
time involved to make this dish. It obviously takes longer to make a real
lemon tart than scoop out bought-in ice cream.

Ask yourself the following after calculating the recipe costs and menu
prices:

- Can the market withstand my pricing?

- What is the competition like?

◆ TOP TIP ◆

If buying an existing business, approach the business figures with caution. They
may not always be as buoyant as they appear. Study them with a fine toothcomb
and ask pertinent questions.

At the beginning of your business, there could be a degree of wastage
which will have an impact on your GP margins, but this will be resolved in
time with good management practices once the business gets going.

Some items will be cheaper than others to prepare. Do offset more expensive dishes by lowering the GP on these dishes and increasing the GP on
the cheaper dishes. For example, it is hard to make 65 per cent GP on
some dishes which use more expensive meat, game, shellfish, fish and foie
gras. This is loss-leader practice and will help to increase the sales of the
more expensive item but shore up the cost by making a larger GP on
cheaper dishes.

Before the net profit is calculated the cost of overheads is deducted from the
gross profit including wages and running costs, leaving you with an average
profit of ten to 15 per cent. Then deduct the loan repayments, interest and tax.

Bear in mind that interest rates can vary, and the amounts paid to
staff, the owner and partners are equally unknown at the initial stage
of the business.

Wine bar/restaurant trading projections

Mon-Thurs	Covers	Cost	Multiply by	Total
Morning café	20	£3	4	£240
T/o lunch*	20	£4.50	4	£360
Lunch	15	£10	4	£600
Evening meal	20	£25	4	£2,000
Wine bar	20	£5.50	4	£440
Total				£3,640

Friday	Covers	Cost	Multiply by	Total
Morning café	30	£3	1	£90
T/o lunch	20	£4.50	1	£90
Lunch	20	£10	1	£200
Evening meal	40	£25	1	£1,000
Wine bar	50	£7.50	1	£375
Total				£1,755

Saturday	Covers	Cost	Multiply by	Total
Morning café	35	£4	1	£140
T/o lunch	10	£4.50	1	£45
Lunch	45	£10	1	£450
Evening meal	45	£25	1	£1,125
Wine bar	50	£10	1	£500
Total				£2,260

Sunday	Covers	Cost	Multiply by	Total
Breakfst/brunch	20	£8.50	1	£170
Lunch	40	£15	1	£600
Wine bar	30	£10	1	£300
Total				£1,070

Total for the week	£8,725
Monthly average	£37,808

*T/0: take out lunch

Monthly costs

Rent/rates	£2,500	Laundry	£300
Wages	£8,000	Breakages	£200
Food	£10,000	Promotion	£500
Wine	£600		
Utilities	£750		
Loan servicing	£2,500		
		Total	£25,350

Monthly average less monthly costs £12,458 less VAT @ 17.5% = £10,602

Cover charges, menu supplement charges and service charges

These charges can sound two alarm bells in customers' minds: once when looking at the menu and seeing extra charges for bread, steep pricing for vegetables and the so-called optional service charge. The next time is when they ask for the bill and see hidden charges added on the total.

You may lose customers in the first instance, as seasoned diners-out can spot those extra charges a mile off while scrutinising the menu. They will think twice about going through your doors. The resentment that is caused will rocket when those hidden charges are there in black and white on the bill. Those customers who feel they have been ripped off will hardly return. Customers naturally prefer to know in advance about all the charges.

Cover charge

The old-fashioned cover charge is sadly alive and well. It is mainly found in tourist hot spots where unsuspecting tourists from here and abroad may not notice it. The restaurant covers itself by saying it is for linen, glasses and staff. Really, any excuse will do. But then that same restaurant will charge for bread and add a service charge. It is an iniquitous charge which I and countless other customers – and, to be fair, many restaurateurs – find totally unacceptable.

Extra charges

A medium-range Portsmouth fish restaurant I have reviewed has a nice little greedy policy: charge them for the sauces to go with the fish, charge them for the bread and the vegetables on already high prices and slap on a 15% service charge.

The price per head for a very dull two-course meal of no particular expertise at this restaurant is the price for a superb three-course set menu with well-chosen produce at Gordon Ramsay's Royal Hospital Road London restaurant at lunchtime. No contest.

Another restaurant in the same area as Gordon Ramsay's has a set menu but many of the dishes featured attract a supplement, boosting the price by some 20–25 per cent on the total bill. This is unacceptable practice. Fine, maybe one or two dishes – the Scotch fillet of beef, the North Sea lobster – will be more expensive to buy in, but with all these supplements it is far better and fairer to have an à la carte menu.

If you feel you must charge for bread then make sure it is excellent bread. If you feel you must charge for any extras, do offer the very best produce if you want repeat business.

Service charge

The service charge is a vexed question and, before we go into it, there is no legal control on how you charge for service. This charge, added to the bill before VAT is added, is usually $12\frac{1}{2}$ per cent of the bill, although it does rise to 15 per cent. The word 'discretionary' usually goes before this percentage. However, most people pay up without fuss and don't query the said service.

This is a very common practice and in lower priced restaurants this may be a fixed amount added to the bill, but in many restaurants it is that $12\frac{1}{2}\%$. Some restaurants pass it on to their staff (waiting and kitchen) if wages are low, and this is promised at the start of employment, or it is seen as part of the revenue if staff are better paid.

Most staff, however, prefer the tips and a distribution of the charge. But, increasingly in this more sophisticated and enlightened eating-out climate, customers are catching on to the fact that if they pay the service charge, they don't leave a tip. Why pay twice? They assume that the service charge is just that: the money going directly to the waiting staff.

Customers are within their rights not to pay the service charge if they have been let down by poor service. This, of course, may not be the fault of the waiting staff but the slowness of the kitchen. My advice is to remove the service charge without quibbling if the customer asks for it.

Voluntary service charges

There is great concern within the hospitality industry that many diners are feeling they have been tricked into paying twice for service by restaurants who leave credit card slips blank for tips. Trading standards officers report that many customers are being caught out because of the widespread use of credit cards.

A survey was done in London by trading standards inspectors who found that half of the 68 restaurants visited left the credit card slip open for a gratuity despite already adding a service charge.

Restaurants that impose voluntary service charges are in breach of a code of practice brought in alongside the Consumer Protection Act 1987 which seeks to abolish the charges and have them incorporated in a single bill.

If restaurants fail to show the cost of eating out clearly and legibly this could result in fines of £5,000. Trading Standards are not looking to ban service charges but want to ensure that customers have a real choice of whether to pay – or not.

Conclusion

An optional service charge is acceptable, but the practice of leaving a credit card slip blank for a tip when the customer has already paid service is not.

A duped customer can see it as one the most objectionable aspects about dining out and it can sour a very good restaurant experience. Avoid following this – sadly, widespread – underhand, greedy practice.

TIPS FOR ATTRACTING FINANCE

To attract financing it pays to have the following:

◆ sales goals;

◆ customer profiles;

◆ economic environment (is there an economic slump or boom?);

◆ knowledge of trends in the restaurant trade;

◆ analysis of competition;

◆ marketing strategy;

◆ key person resumés – you and your partner'(s) strengths and background;

◆ your chef's background and expertise (if you have a chef on board);

◆ cash flow projection;

◆ revenue projections;

◆ taxes – VAT included;

◆ financing requirements: amount needed, detailed budget, repayment options;

◆ bank documents.

Again, this vital paperwork need to be well presented in relevant titled folders and handed out with confidence.

RAISING CAPITAL AND BUSINESS PARTNERS/INVESTORS

Aim to raise more money than you need. You often have only one chance of raising money so take a close look at what you think you will need. It is very difficult to ask the same source the second time around for more funding. If your figures are too conservative it may ultimately mean that your business proposition is not viable.

Raising the money

The bank is not your only port of call. There could be better and cheaper ways of raising finance. Work out exactly how much you need and for how long. Re-mortgaging your house (should you have the luxury of owning one) would not be suitable if you need money for the short-term. If you need money to buy equipment do look at renting and leasing options.

If you do choose to go down the bank route, shop around. The competition between banks to do business with you can be buoyant so you may be able to afford to look around at the deals on offer. But negotiate too. Don't accept the proposals for what they are. Stipulate your needs and offer a rate of interest to the time you can start paying back the loan. It never hurts to ask.

However, banks can be wary of lending money to new restaurant ventures as the track record is less than successful.

There is no rule to say that you have to bank with the bank that gives you a loan. Perhaps there are better deals at another bank. And if the loan comes from a bank that doesn't have a high street presence or is too far away from your business to make it practical to pay money in, for example, then this is yet another reason for banking elsewhere. And the bank which has lent you the money will respect your good business sense.

WORKING IN A PARTNERSHIP

Are you going into business alone or with a partner? Or will you be forming a company with investors or lenders? The latter is the route taken by most small restaurants. Try to achieve majority control with partners or investors as minor shareholders. But you have to convince them that you are capable of running such a business.

Keep the people who matter in the know. Your partners – should you have any – must be completely up to date with any transactions you may have made on behalf of the business. Communication is all when dealing with partners, and those who fund your restaurant, if you wish to stay in business.

Choose your partners or investors with great care and thought. Discuss your plans in great detail. Are they on the same wavelength as you? Do they have the same aspirations and goals? What strengths do they possess? Be aware of the investor who wishes to run the business because he or she knows better. This can only lead to tears and a messy falling-out. Look for investors and/or partners who respect your strengths and weaknesses and vice versa. Clearly define the areas of responsibility at the onset. These may shift as the business progresses but do discuss these changes in full when they arise.

When entering into a partnership, outline and protect personal investment as well as the agreed split of assets and liabilities. Get it down on paper and get a lawyer. See Legal Tips in this chapter.

CAPITAL EXPENDITURE

Let's look at the capital costs before the search for funding begins and work out figures for each cost. Remember, if your figures are too conservative, it is difficult to return to the same source for more funding. There will be guesswork involved as not all figures can be established correctly, hence a contingency fund is needed.

The property
The lists below for capital expenditure for a restaurant/bar can be made specific and appropriate to your business:

◆ rent deposit, on-going rent or cost to buy;

◆ renovations including labour and materials;

◆ building costs and labour;

◆ plumbing, electrical labour and materials;

◆ décor including any artefacts;

- toilet upgrade;

- accountant's and bookkeeper's fees;

- bar construction and furbishing;

- chairs, tables, service area costs;

- floor covering, window blinds/curtains;

- lighting;

- heating, air conditioning, kitchen extractor fan;

- fire extinguishers.

Kitchen and restaurant equipment

You may need:

- kitchen equipment large and small including rental equipment costs;

- glass, cutlery, crockery;

- coffee espresso machine – lease or buy;

- cleaning costs including vacuum cleaners, window cleaners;

- rubbish removal costs;

- linen, napkins, glass cloths, kitchen uniforms, waiting staff uniforms;

- laundry costs;

- music system, speakers, recorded music and performing rights costs;

- cash register;

- opening stocks: food, alcohol, cleaning materials;

- opening party costs.

Ancillary costs

These will include:

- telephones;

- gas and electricity;

- office equipment;

- printing for menus, cards, publicity handouts, bill heads;

- advertising;

- promotion;

- graphics;

- menu research including travel;

- exterior lighting and menu boards.

Accountancy and other costs including legal fees
Budget for:

- accountant's and bookkeeper's fees;

- legal fees;

- rates;

- insurance;

- permits: fire, health, business licence;

- licence fees;

- staff costs – waiting, kitchen, cleaning, office;

- breakages;

- operating capital;

- contingency fund.

NEXT STEPS IN FINDING FUNDING

With your capital cost figures under your belt, and armed with a business plan and your initial trading proposal worked out, it's time to persuade others to fund your venture.

Whether the capital is via the bank or a private investor, the lender is looking for the survival of the business in order to recoup the loan and the agreed interest.

The lender needs to be satisfied that the business has the right people at the helm, its location is sound and that good research into the projected customer base has been undertaken.

Bookkeeping and accountancy

It is essential to initiate good bookkeeping practices from the beginning of the business so that investors, accountants and the Inland Revenue can see at a glance the cash flow, expenses, and profit and loss margins.

Place all transactions on computer as this will give the restaurateur immediate information on the operation: the sales, its mix, stock turnover, sales per table and waiter (very useful for checking facts if needed), food and drink cost percentages.

Computers also offer a cost-effective way of reducing paperwork but bookkeeping (nowadays usually put on a software package) is still essential, so do add the cost of employing a bookkeeper/accountant into the capital costs.

Choose an accountant who has experience and a liking for the restaurant trade. Do a cashflow forecast together.

Bookkeeping and accountancy requirements

Record cash and bank records, weekly sales of all aspects of the business (food and alcohol sales for example) and weekly payments (suppliers, wages, rent etc).

Record the weekly income and expenditure on printouts or summary sheets so that management can see at a glance where the money is going out and coming in.

The accountant will also require information regarding VAT, tips, credit card and cash sales, wages, purchases, operating costs (rent, rates, utilities, telephone, laundry for example), drawings for investors and owners and capital costs (maintenance, repairs, improvements).

This analysis of breaking down the business into the sum of its parts can be of immense help to see where the business is going, its strengths and weaknesses, its seasonal swings. It can also be helpful in combating fraud and theft. See tips, page 54.

At the end of the financial year (March 31), two summaries need to be prepared: the trading profit and loss accounts showing the gross profit, and the net profit and the balance sheet showing the company's financial position. The latter shows the assets owned and the debts owed. The difference between the two is the capital value of the business, representing the capital invested by the owner/investors and the retained profits.

VAT

Value Added Tax (VAT) is a tax charged on most business transactions made in the UK or the Isle of Man. Some see the restaurateur and other business men and women as perhaps unpaid government tax collectors.

VAT is also charged on goods and some services imported from places outside the European Union, and on goods and some services coming into the UK from the other EU countries.

All goods and services that are VAT rated are called 'taxable supplies'. You must charge VAT on your taxable supplies from the date you first need to be registered. The value of these supplies is called your 'taxable turnover'.

There are currently three rates of VAT:

- 17.5% – standard-rated supplies on most goods and services

- 5% – reduced-rate supplies on fuel and power used in the home and by charities

- 0% – zero-rated supplies which are non-chargeable. Examples are most food, books, newspapers and children's clothing.

Registering for VAT

You must register for VAT if you are in business and your taxable turnover, not just your profit, goes over a certain limit.

The current VAT registration threshold is £58,000 (October 2004) but you can opt to register for VAT if your taxable turnover (the amount going through the business, not just the profit) is less than this, if what you do counts as a business for VAT purposes.

If your taxable turnover is below the limit you can apply for voluntary registration if you can prove what you do is a business for VAT purposes.

The benefits of registration under the limit include increased credibility for your business but, once you are registered, you will have to account for output tax on all your taxable supplies which are not zero rated. But also, you can take credit for any input tax on those taxable supplies.

You will also have to send in VAT returns regularly and keep proper records and accounts so that VAT officers can examine them if necessary.

VAT accounting

For small businesses, there are a number of simplified arrangements to make VAT accounting easier:

- **Cash accounting**: if your taxable turnover is under £600,000 a year you can arrange to account to Customs for VAT on the basis of cash received and paid rather than the invoice date or time of supply.

- **Annual accounting**: if your turnover is under £660,00 a year you can join the annual accounting scheme and send in just one return a year, rather than the quarterly returns which most businesses do.

- **Bad debt relief**: if you supply goods or services to a customer but you are not paid, you may be able to claim relief from VAT on the debts.

- **Flat rate scheme**: you may be eligible if your turnover is under £150,000. It helps save on administration due to not accounting internally for VAT on each individual 'in and out'. Payment is over a set percentage of the total turnover.

Ten top tips for simplifying VAT for small businesses

1. Registering for VAT may have major implications on your pricing structure so always calculate these into any costings.

2. Apply to register in plenty of time so that you get the help available to you, and also get your VAT number in good time for printing onto cards, invoices etc and for other purposes.

3. Be clear about the impact of VAT on your growing business turnover.

4. Good bookkeeping is vital for overall business management. Check documents you receive. You must have a VAT invoice to claim back VAT. A statement is not a proper invoice.

5. Always enter cash receipts in your books before using the cash to make purchases.

6. Many businesses take advantage of the VAT they've collected, making it work for them before being paid to Customs. Pay the VAT into a separate bank account to accumulate interest. Be sure to keep the VAT collections for payment only to Customs and Excise and not for other purposes.

7. If you find yourself unable to send your VAT return or cheque on time call Customs on 0845 010 9000 and tell them why.

8. Consider making a part payment to reduce the surcharge payment.

9. Always quote your VAT number on correspondence or delays/confusion will occur.

10. If you are not sure, ask. It's in both your and Customs and Excise's interests. If in doubt, shout!

PAYROLL

Records must be kept of all staff, whether full or part-time. Avoid the temptation to pay unrecorded cash for labour as penalties for income fraud are severe. The following are necessary to keep records:

◆ name and address of employee;

◆ their tax code number and National Insurance number;

◆ tips earned: restaurateurs are responsible for all income earned, tips included;

◆ tax inspectors can estimate tip earnings if no service charge is included.

INSURANCE

Insurance is a very simple concept. Your annual payment will provide cover for your business which needs insurance for building, contents and liability, the latter for any litigation (dispute, lawsuit brought against the business, for example).

Even if you are able to cover the costs of replacement or repair or any loss that may occur, such as a shelf giving way with a hundred plates tumbling to the floor, it would be irresponsible not to be insured against any problems regarding guests' legal actions.

Your biggest risk may be from the customers themselves, however delightful, with items being broken or simply taken. This does apply too to staff. There is also the possibility of customers or staff falling in your restaurant, and the building itself needing monitoring for safety.

Insurance details to look out for

The duty of disclosure is vitally important when confirming and agreeing to the conditions of the policy. The insurer must know what you wish to cover as the type of policy required must be an accurate reflection of your business. Be clear and specific and ask for written confirmation in all areas of your cover. Ask your local authority about insurance requirements.

Do spend time and effort talking to the right insurers – ie those dealing in restaurant/hotel businesses – and getting several quotes. Or get in touch with an insurance broker. Ask those who are in the restaurant business who they might recommend to receive quotes from. Ask questions. And factor the cost of insurance into your overall costings.

Public liability

Public liability covers injury and property damage caused by your personal negligence and/or business negligence.

Product liability

Product liability relates to any products you provide but specifically to food you serve, either bought-in or cooked on the premises. Should a customer find a nail in a roll (yes, it happened to me), you are liable.

Manager liability

Manager liability covers you for staff looking after customers in the absence of the owner. Customers, when in sueing mood, will not only sue you and your business but also the staff representing you at the time.

Getting the right cover

Your policy must include fire, storm, tempest (however ancient this terminology is), burglary, malicious damage, glass and other covers.

Additional cover which you may wish to consider is business interruption which replaces lost income in the event of a claim where your business is interrupted. Generally figures are based on your yearly income. This could be because of physical damage to your property and replaces lost income when you are unable to function as a restaurant.

Do ask for cover which guarantees you payment on a weekly basis for cash flow purposes and not payment once the claim is known some months after the event.

Obviously be aware that if your business is your sole income, bills need to be paid regardless of an interruption to your restaurant. Payments should be made until normal business can proceed and you have regained the income you would normally expect. These are based on last year's figures for the time of year and not necessarily during your busiest period. Even when the work to repair or replace is complete, it should pay on a descending scale until your business returns to normal.

Your building and contents insurance should reflect all contents and all buildings independent of one another. Insurance is based on replacing and repairing, not on the market value or saleable value, so ask a builder or valuer to provide you with an estimate. Then add a percentage on to this figure for removal of debris, architect's fees (if applicable) and any other costs.

◆ TOP TIP ◆

An insurance policy is a legal, binding contract with terms and conditions, so it is up to you to make sure that all items you wish to insure are covered.

A workers' compensation policy should be discussed with your insurer. If you have a personal accident and sickness/income policy it is advisable to continue with this.

Fraud and theft in the restaurant business

Look out for the following:

◆ Short-changing and overcharging.

◆ Issuing food without an order – complicity between kitchen and waiting staff.

◆ Deleting an order as a 'no sale' or cancelled order and pocketing the money.

◆ Stock sold for cash.

◆ Selling stock to other businesses.

◆ Use of stolen credit cards.

◆ Running off more than one transaction at a time for the same sale.

◆ Suppliers adding the date into the total, short-weighing and overcharging.

◆ Suppliers delivering short orders and charging for complete order.

◆ Theft of food, drink, equipment and money by staff.

To combat this some large restaurants are installing CCTV cameras over tills. Do install automated till systems. Stocktake regularly. Having a fool-proof system against fraud is not possible so be vigilant.

CREDIT CARDS

In today's market, payment by card is the preferred method of payment. In 2003, the number of credit cards in the UK payment markets was the highest ever recorded and more than half of all adults regularly made debit card purchases.

Accepting credit cards brings the following benefits to your business:

- More customers through your door if they see their card is accepted.

- No cash restrictions can mean that customers spend more.

- An increased turnover and profit.

- Your banking becomes automated, making procedures simpler and faster.

Our increasingly cashless society demands the use of credit and debit cards in most restaurants, although some quick turnaround restaurants only work on cash as card costs are too high to merit the expense.

Negotiate charges with the card companies and renegotiate those charges a year after trading. They may see a good, profitable company in the making and wish to partake of your success long-term.

LEGAL TIPS

Don't put your personal assets at risk

If you are starting a business with one or more people, you can choose partnership, limited liability partnership or limited company status. In a partnership all partners are jointly liable for debts. If you come up against a legal problem you will be risking your personal assets.

Put it in writing

Do put all your business deals and agreements in writing. If you have a verbal agreement get confirmation in writing. A verbal one is often difficult to put into effect if problems arise. A written record will also prevent people from trying to change their minds or giving you a different story at a later stage.

It pays to get advice early on

Get legal advice early on as it will pay in the long run. Problems can arise in the long-term if this is neglected. Ask for an estimate of the cost if you seek a lawyer's advice. If forming a company, shop around for a solicitor's package deal.

Get someone to recommend a solicitor

Solicitors specialise in many areas of the law and there are many different types of law so this can be a daunting step. Recommendations from other companies are a good start. Do ask solicitors for testimonials and references and follow these up.

Keep up to date with changes in the law

Employment law is constantly changing so keep up to date. Every employer must provide a statement of employment clearly laying down certain details. It can be in your interests to include policies that are not needed by law to safeguard you.

BUSINESS ADVICE ORGANISATIONS

Business Debtline

Of course, the hope is that good finance and accountancy practices have been adhered to from the beginning in putting your business together. But there may be worrying times when some good, practical advice from experts would help enormously. The psychological boost of just talking to someone who deals with financial problems is quite energising.

Contact Business Debtline (0800 197 6026), a national telephone service that offers free, confidential and independent advice to small businesses on tackling cashflow problems by:

◆ preparing a budget for your business;

◆ prioritising all your debts;

◆ dealing with court proceedings;

◆ understanding bankruptcy;

◆ avoiding repossession of your home and business;

◆ dealing with tax matters;

◆ negotiating with creditors and bailiffs and dealing with most other debt and cashflow issues that you and your business may face.

Federation of Small Businesses

The Federation of Small Businesses is the leading organisation for small businesses in the UK and campaigns on their behalf to improve the financial and economic environment in which they operate. Alongside this influential lobbying, FSB members also enjoy a unique protection and benefits package providing instant access to legal and professional advice and support.

For further details visit their website: www.fsb.org.uk

Other organisations

There are two other useful contacts as well as government agencies and organisations that can help you make the right business decisions.

The Small Business Service (SBS) is an organisation which operates a number of schemes and initiatives that are designed to help small businesses in a variety of ways. They encourage businesses to be more innovative and to exploit new technologies, help get finance more readily, and can provide ways for businesses to measure and improve efficiency. Their website is www.business.link.gov.uk

The SBS also oversees the work of the network of local Business Link offices that operate throughout England. Similar services are Business Gateway for Lowland Scotland, Business Information Source in Highland Scotland, Business Connect in Wales and the Local Economic Development Unit for Northern Ireland.

The Business Links provide independent and impartial advice, information and a range of services to help small firms and those starting up new businesses. Call Business Link on (0845) 600 9006.

The British Chamber of Commerce (BCC) is the national face of the UK's network of accredited Chambers of Commerce, and campaigns to reduce burdens on business and create a more favourable business environment. For further help contact the BCC's website: www.britishchambers.org.uk

5

Running a Safe Business

Running a safe, hygienic business is one of the biggest tests a restaurateur has to deal with. This chapter covers the restaurant's food hygiene, staff handling of the food, adhering to strict hygiene standards and the premises themselves.

This chapter gives an outline of the Food Safety Act, the Food Premises Regulations, food hygiene training, temperature controls, and foods that need chilling and those that don't. The various types of food poisoning are outlined, and there is also advice on staff hygiene, environmental health requirements and the visit by an inspector.

FOOD SAFETY REGULATIONS

The Food Safety Act 1990

Under this Act you must not:

◆ Sell food (or keep for sale) anything that is unfit for people to eat.

◆ Cause food to be dangerous to health.

◆ Sell food that is not what the customer is entitled to expect, in terms of content or quality.

◆ Describe or present food in a way that is false or misleading.

Food Premises (Registration) Regulations 1991

Under this act you must:

◆ Register your business at least 28 days before opening a new food business.

◆ Contact your local authority for the appropriate (and very straightforward) form. There is no charge.

Food Safety (General Food Hygiene) Regulations 1995

Food hygiene training:

◆ Regulations made under the Food Safety Act require that all persons who handle open food in the course of a food business receive food hygiene training.

◆ Short course levels are foundation, intermediate and advanced. Find out what courses are available from your local authority.

Food Safety (Temperature Control) Regulations 1995

This covers:

◆ The temperature at which certain foods must be kept.

◆ Which foods are exempt from specific temperature control.

◆ When the regulations allow flexibility.

In Scotland the regulations are slightly different to the rest of the UK but the principles are the same. Contact your local authority.

♦ TOP TIP ♦

Foods that need temperature control must be kept either:

HOT at or above 63°C
COLD at or below 8°C

FOOD STORAGE

Foods that need chilling

Foods that need chilling include:

♦ Milk, yoghurt, cream, butter, foods with cream filling, dairy-based desserts and certain cheeses.

♦ Many cooked products until ready to eat cold or heated. Most foods containing eggs, meat, fish, dairy products, cereals, rice, pulses or vegetables and sandwich fillings containing these ingredients.

♦ Most smoked or cured products like hams unless the curing method means the product is not perishable at room temperature.

♦ Prepared ready-to-eat meals including prepared vegetables, salad leaves, coleslaw and products containing mayonnaise.

♦ Pizzas with meat, fish or vegetables.

♦ Foods with 'use by' and 'keep refrigerated' labels.

Foods that don't need chilling

These include:

♦ Some cured/smoked products.

♦ Bakery goods.

♦ Canned and dried foods like pickles, jams, sauces, though these do need chilling once opened.

Mail order food

Mail order food must not be transported at temperatures that could cause a health risk. Therefore food that needs chilling should be delivered by chilled compartment vehicle.

Fridge storage and temperature control

Meat storage at the base of the fridge is the rule to adhere to. A full guide can be obtained from your local authority. The fridge temperature should be between 1C and 4C to stop bacteria from multiplying. Keep a thermometer in the fridge and record a diary of temperatures for health and safety inspection. Keep it on the door to remind staff to check the temperature levels.

FOOD POISONING AND AVOIDING CONTAMINATION

As a restaurateur you and your staff need to understand what causes food poisoning and how it can be avoided. It is vital that your restaurant is clean throughout. The kitchen is naturally the hot spot where cleanliness is of paramount importance. The food you serve must be absolutely safe and, by strict following of hygiene and cross contamination rules, this will be achieved.

There are four micro-organisms that are the most common causes of food poisoning which, of course, make for alarming reading. But they are preventable.

Campylobactor

This is the most common food poisoning bug in the UK. It is found in raw and undercooked poultry, red meat, unpasteurised milk and untreated water. Just a piece of undercooked chicken can cause severe illness.

Symptoms: gastroenteritis with fever, abdominal cramps and diarrhoea that is often bloody. Can be fatal.

Salmonella

The second most common food poisoning bug. It can be found in eggs, raw meat, poultry, unpasteurised milk, yeast and even pasta, coconut and chocolate. Salmonella grows very well in the food itself unless the food is chilled. It is also passed easily from person to person by poor hygiene such as not washing hands.

Symptoms: usually mild, with abdominal pain, diarrhoea and nausea but rarely vomiting.

Clostridium perfringens

The third most common bug and the least reported as symptoms are vague. Found in soil, sewage, animal manure and in the guts of animals and humans. Food cooked slowly in large quantities then left to stand for a long time is its breeding ground.

Symptoms: when taken in large numbers, the bacteria produce toxins which attack the gut lining, causing diarrhoea and acute abdominal pain.

Listeria

This is a food poisoning bug of particular danger to pregnant women, babies and the elderly. It is found in soft, mould-ripened cheeses, patés, unpasteurised milk and shellfish. Listeria resists heat, salt and nitrate and acidity better than many micro-organisms.

Symptoms: fever, headache, nausea and vomiting. Can be fatal to the elderly, immune impaired infants and developing foetuses.

Scrombotoxin

Although not strictly speaking a bug, this poison is produced by certain bacteria in oily fish which has been allowed to spoil through inadequate refrigeration. It causes a dramatic histamine reaction. Scrombotoxin is found in fresh and tinned mackerel, tuna and – very rarely – Swiss cheese.

Symptoms: tingling or burning in the mouth, a rash on the face or upper body, itching, sweating and headache with a drop in blood pressure, abdominal pain, diarrhoea and vomiting.

E.coli 0157

Most strains of E.coli are harmless but those producing the poison verocy-toxin can cause severe illness, E.coli 0157 being one. It is found in farm animals and land contaminated with their faeces, and transmitted through undercooked minced beef (such as burgers) and raw, inadequately or con-taminated milk.

Symptoms: abdominal cramps and bloody diarrhoea. In serious cases kidney failure, severe anaemia, neurological problems and death.

In order to combat food poisoning obtain good clear advice from your local authority health inspector. All of the above are perfectly possible to prevent if you are aware of them and how they can be avoided. Poisonings by salmonella and campylobactor are, however, on the increase due to a lack of understanding by those handling food.

Preventing food poisoning

Lack of common sense also features in food poisoning. Leaving raw chicken out in a hot kitchen for four hours without covering it is asking for trouble. It should have been refrigerated, of course. Preparing a sandwich on a board which has just been used for cutting up raw duck breasts is another action to avoid. Keeping a bottle of milk on a hot window ledge throughout the day will surely result in mild discomfort or worse if drunk.

Heavy-duty plastic or polypropylene colour-coded boards must also be used in a commercial kitchen, and thoroughly scrubbed in hot, soapy water and rinsed after use to avoid cross-contamination and food poisoning. Or use an antibacterial spray with kitchen towel.

A well-publicised case of food poisoning by a caterer at a wedding who left the entire buffet laid out in a hot marquee for over four hours, while pictures of the happy couple were being taken, resulted in mass serious poisoning.

If space is at a premium in the fridges you may have to re-think your menu and your ordering if some items cannot be refrigerated for any length of time.

Eggs

Eggs have been under scrutiny for many years. Health and safety guide-lines suggest that raw or semi-cooked eggs may pose a salmonella food poisoning problem. All recipes printed in newspapers, magazines and books carry a warning not to serve undercooked eggs to the elderly or women who are pregnant (see food poisoning list: listeria).

So out of the window may go some of the most wonderful egg dishes such as eggs Benedict, poached or lightly scrambled eggs and Hollandaise sauce. It is up to you whether to make this decision to serve eggs that aren't thoroughly cooked.

You may wish to add a note on the menu saying that particular dishes con-tain lightly cooked or raw egg to inform your customers and safeguard your interests but it is seen over the top by some.

STAFF HYGIENE

Staff must always wash their hands with soap and clean towels after using the toilet. Hand washing must also take place to avoid cross contamination after handling raw poultry, for example. Even if kitchen staff nip out to the restaurant to check on a booking, for example, they must wash their hands before resuming work with food.

Staff must be introduced to other personal hygiene matters too: fingers touching the face, nose, ears, hair or other parts of the body while working is unacceptable as this can spread infection and micro-organisms. Wearing a hat is a sensible option too for kitchen staff.

Waiting staff too must wash their hands before starting work and abide by the personal hygiene rules as mentioned above. There is no easy solution for management to discern whether or not their staff wash their hands after visiting the toilet. However, a reminder of this essential step is one way of getting the message across.

I am constantly amazed by my own observations in queuing for loos in public places how few people actually wash their hands before going out of the door. This essential step should be practised whether or not the person is in the catering industry.

Cloths

Dishcloths and other cloths in the kitchen are one of the prime suspects in spreading germs. Use non-woven dishcloths rather than sponges as there are fewer traps for germs. Sponges also hold more water where bacteria can thrive.

Don't even think of using a cloth which is used on a counter to mop up the floor then used again for surface tops. Disinfect cloths in bleach regularly and dry flat, not scrunched up. Be a devil and throw them away after quite extensive use!

Change tea towels and hand towels often.

ENVIRONMENTAL HEALTH

Have you talked to environmental health officers about required standards for running a restaurant? This should be done when you are looking at premises to get a clear picture of the requirements. Some properties may not be at all suitable or be able to be changed to fit the required standards. Contact your local authority for advice.

Environmental health requirements

Restaurant kitchens take a physical hammering, and the effort needed to promote the best standards of hygiene, cleanliness, stock care and food rotation is a constant one. Take your eye off the ball – and your staff – and you could land up with a big problem with food poisoning. Witness Gordon Ramsay's television programme *Kitchen Nightmares* to see how poorly run some restaurant kitchens can be due either to laziness or lack of knowledge.

The role of the environmental health officer

The policing of standards is down to environmental health officers from local councils who enforce the law and, although the perception by some in the trade is one of draconian laws and over-the-top requirements, the system can't be bucked. Some of the requests are legally binding, others aren't. But their advice can be invaluable, particularly for those starting up in the business or those whose standards have slipped.

EHOs can, by law, turn up unannounced at all reasonable hours and proceed to inspect your restaurant kitchen, toilets, storage space, the restaurant itself and your rubbish area. They may also visit due to a complaint.

Some of the many items they will inspect are lids and labels on containers, the use of the right chopping boards, fridge and freezer temperatures. They will take a keen interest in the suitability and cleanliness of tiles, floor, walls and ceilings, storage, hand basins for staff, how raw and cooked meat are stored in the fridge, air circulation and vermin problems.

There are EHO horror stories: stoves with no knobs on, meaning staff turning the gas on with pliers, dirty stale oil left in fryers and filthy fridges with no labelling on containers. They have also discovered babies' soiled nappies left in the kitchen, mould and mice droppings behind equipment, fire doors propped open with unsealed rubbish, and cleaning fluids transferred to lemonade bottles.

EHO inspection
This is what you can expect when your business is inspected.

Inspection:

◆ The inspector will show identification.

◆ A routine inspection will be carried out.

◆ Some premises can be inspected every six months, others much less often.

◆ Feedback will be given such as information about identified hazards and guidance on how they can be avoided.

◆ You will be given the reasons in writing for any action you are asked to take.

◆ Where there is an apparent breach of law, you will receive a statement of what that law is.

◆ A reasonable time to meet statutory requirements is given except when there is an immediate risk to public health.

◆ You are entitled to be informed of the procedures for appealing against local authority action.

Inspectors' powers:

◆ They can take samples, photographs and inspect records.

◆ They may write informally to put right any problems they find.

◆ Where breaches of the law are identified which must be put right they may serve you with an improvement order.

◆ They can detain or seize goods.

◆ In serious cases they may decide to recommend a prosecution.

◆ If there is an imminent health risk to consumers, inspectors can serve an emergency prohibition order backed up by the court which forbids the use of the premises or equipment.

If you disagree with the outcome contact your local authority's head of environmental health or trading standards services to see if the matter can be resolved informally. If disagreement remains contact your local councillor.

Contact your local authority or trade association if you think the law is being applied differently to other authorities. Ask about LACOTS (Local Authorities Co-ordinating Body on Food and Trading Standards).

You have the right of appeal to a magistrates' court against an improvement notice or a refusal by a local authority to lift an emergency prohibition order made earlier by the court. A magistrates' court must confirm the emergency closure of a business or the seizure of food. If magistrates decide premises have been shut down without proper reason or food has been wrongly seized or detained, you have a right to compensation.

Other considerations:

◆ The past history of the offence.

◆ The seriousness of the offence.

◆ The inspectors' confidence in the restaurant's management.

◆ The consequences of non-compliance.

◆ The attitude of the operator/proprietor.

◆ **TOP TIP** ◆

Your local authority is ready to help if you need any advice on food safety.

Trade associations and independent consultancy services can also help.

6

Design and Equipment for Kitchen and Restaurant

Careful design defines how functional the overall restaurant and kitchen can be. This chapter deals with the design of the hall, the bar and the restaurant itself. It will also help you with the choice of chairs, tables, and give tips on flooring, walls and ceilings, toilets, lighting and how to dress a restaurant table from top to toe.

This chapter also looks at what to look out for in kitchen design and kitchen equipment, from a lemon squeezer to a fridge and stove. China, glass, cutlery and that all-important service from kitchen to restaurant and back again wraps the chapter up.

DESIGN

Restaurants can be described like this: the kitchen is the factory, the restaurant is the sales office and showroom. Once you accept this more hard-headed approach, the better the planning and the outcome will be.

Restaurant design has changed considerably since the 1990s thrust design into the limelight. Professional designers mostly design with the wow factor in mind, especially in corporate restaurant businesses. All that metal. All that 'leather' seating. All that minimalist lighting. And, to my mind, they all look the same.

But is it necessary to go down the professional designer route to achieve a style or, most importantly, a friendly, accessible, smart environment which is pleasing to the eye? The restaurant's interior – and exterior – will convey to the public your taste, your style. So how do you go about it? Give a professional designer a brief or will it be a DIY job?

Professional design

Seek out some professional expertise before leaping into the unknown, or visit restaurants to pick up on some of the traits you wish to incorporate in your own. But beware of clashing styles or a cluttered look. An integrated overall style has to emerge. Beware too of designs that do not focus on customers' and staff's basic needs, such as comfort and the ability to move around the area to serve at tables. The look has to be in proportion to the space.

Thankfully, swirling carpet patterns, drab curtains and heavy furnishings are mostly in the past. Design now focuses on light walls, wood floors, brightness in furnishings and clever lighting. But often there is little individuality that emerges, with no particular stamp of the owner to make it more personal.

DIY design

How is individuality achieved? If you count on the design only, leaving out the welcoming personality of the owner or manager and good, friendly service with a smile and quality food, the restaurant won't stand out from the crowd. You need all three to create an environment.

Resist the urge to put up artefacts brought back from that memorable holiday in Turkey and Mexico or wherever unless they fit into the overall design. Equally, resist the homey high street chain store look as it will be instantly recognisable. As my then 2-year old son was wheeled around in his pushchair in a John Lewis department store, pointing to furniture and lighting we had at home, 'we got one of those'...'and those'...'and those', your customers will also recognise their provenance. Customers rarely wish to sit in a restaurant that resembles their home. They can do that quite easily with a takeaway *chez eux.*

Also, these products may not be robust enough to withstand the hard wear and tear demanded in a public space, so a visit to a specialist restaurant furniture shop and commercial kitchen business should be considered.

But design can be just as effective for the neighbourhood restaurant or the gastro pub if it recognises its clientele and goes down the simplest route with no apparent design or expensive furnishings. The owners instead cobble together pine tables and wooden chairs to achieve a look which is inviting to many people, thanks to its approachability. The look also says 'inexpensive meal out.' However, looks can be deceiving.

As a guide, an allowance of $2\frac{1}{2}$–4 square metres per person in the restaurant takes into consideration seating, table space, gangway and access to bar/counter.

Let's look at the layout and practicality of the premises.

IS YOUR RESTAURANT FUNCTIONAL?

No matter how quirky or charming a restaurant is, it must be first and foremost **functional**: rule number one. When looking at properties, look at the space from the point of view of being full. Working at full tilt. Not just a few tables taken with staff ambling through. Imagine your restaurant with every table taken. Buzzing.

Now walk through the space from its entrance to the back of the restaurant and note the following:

◆ Is the shape of the property conducive to running a business? Or is the shape too awkward, the ceiling too low, creating huge noise levels?

◆ Is there a flow for customers and staff to reach tables comfortably? To get to the toilets? For staff to access the kitchen and bar?

◆ What is the signage like outside and inside? Do these need improving?

◆ Is the entrance welcoming, accommodating, well lit? Is the door handle user-friendly or do your customers have to fight to get in?

◆ Is the entrance draught-free? Customers will not return if their table is in direct line of a blast of cold air. A double door lobby is one answer.

◆ Where are the light switches for staff on entry? If you or they have to crash around a dark restaurant to turn the lights on it could be hazardous.

◆ Is there a good cloakroom area for coats, shopping bags, umbrellas? When full to bursting, will this area be another battleground for entry into the restaurant if by the main entrance? If so, can you solve this problem by placing coats elsewhere (but not near tables as coats on pegs brushing against customers' heads is not acceptable).

◆ Is there a large enough entry to take in deliveries? Or is there a good, accessible entry point at the back of the property?

◆ Make a list of any improvements to decoration, signage, lighting and flooring that need to be made.

THE HALL AND BAR

Make your entrance welcoming and uncluttered so that the customer has easy access into the restaurant and so that you can see and greet the customer.

If you have space the bar is an invaluable area, not only for its instant appeal to drinkers on entering the restaurant, but it also functions as a service area. It acts as a control for ordering, making bills out, housing the cash register, taking bookings, making phone calls to suppliers, a focal point for staff, a place to sit down when doing paperwork, storing paperwork and records, plus menu and wine list storage.

The bar may store a percentage of your wines and other drinks, plus glasses, ice, perhaps a glass washer and sink and other items for drinks service. Place racks at the back of the bar for wine storage. And keep it stocked up as it adds to presentation as well as being practical.

♦ TOP TIP ♦

Keep the bar as uncluttered as possible as it is the focal point of the restaurant. And keep it spotless.

The bar is useful for drinks sales as it displays what you have on offer and may also house a coffee machine. Or should I say 'should'. Good coffee is now expected and I would urge new restaurants to invest in an espresso machine. These can be leased or bought. It adds atmosphere as well as the promise of a well-made cup of coffee and is a money-maker as all the Caffe Nero's, Starbucks *et al* will testify to.

If you have no space for a bar you will need to find room elsewhere for making out bills, opening wine, storing menus and all that goes with the smooth running of a restaurant. But, of course, there are places that do not need a bar, such as the country house restaurant or café.

THE RESTAURANT

Tables

The flow. The flow. This is your mantra when designing any part of the restaurant. But first, what type is your restaurant: casual; more formal; a quick lunch place; a big spend restaurant? How much per head do you expect to make? These are crucial questions to ask as they determine your type of table, the space in between, the comfort or otherwise of your chair for a longer or quick meal, where you place your bar and any service stations.

Do you go for round, square or rectangular tables seating two, four, six and eight? Tables with legs or pedestals? Interchangeable round tops? Get accurate measurements of tables and chairs from a variety of manufacturers and place markers or string around the restaurant before committing yourself to buying the furniture. It may not fit in and give you maximum seating with plenty of flow. And it may be too bulky a look, making your restaurant look like a furniture show room.

♦ 76 cm square table seats two.

♦ 1 metre square table seats four.

♦ 1 metre round table seats four.

♦ 1.52 metre round table seats eight.

♦ 137 x 76 cm rectangular table seats four.

If you have a designer it may be possible to have a graphic design or a scale model to play around with.

Do you choose tables that don't require a tablecloth or ones that do? Put under-padding under tablecloths for extra luxury and to safeguard the surface.

♦ TOP TIP ♦

Choose robust tables. They will last.

Stay flexible

The more flexible your seating, the more individual requirements for parties you will be able to offer. The whole restaurant may be booked by a single party and you need to know how many you can seat comfortably and with reasonable staff access to each seat.

Obviously round tables can create problems with large parties as they can't be joined together. But you can buy tables with differing lift-off top sizes and shapes so that you are able to be as flexible as possible.

Flow paths must be maintained from kitchen to tables and from bar to tables. How accessible are the toilets?

Tables by the kitchen door are to be avoided at all costs. That swinging door nearby, a constant flow of staff and noise just aren't acceptable. Not for nothing is this table known in the trade as Siberia. Instead, use this inhospitable space for a service station which houses napkins, cutlery, bread, condiments, candle holders and other items of use for staff to minimise their entry into the kitchen. This can be waist high with several shelves or a simple wooden table.

Chairs

Ah, the vexed question of chairs. The more formal the dining, the longer the customer will stay. The last thing you want to do is to have shifting, uncomfortable customers so a good upholstered chair is essential.

Beware high backs, arm rests and bulky design if you have a small restaurant as they will be taking up valuable space, and look like a furniture warehouse. They must be practical too if the whole restaurant is taken over for a party and must fit the space.

Avoid making a costly mistake by choosing chairs for their aesthetic qualities. They may look elegant and smart but are they up to the job of comfortably and securely holding the increasing girth of the nation? Can they withstand the wear and tear of a busy restaurant? They must be of excellent quality unless you wish to foot the bill for having them repaired or, worse still, disintregate with a customer still seated on one.

Points to consider:

♦ Either ask a manufacturer to come up with a design to suit your restaurant or choose chairs from a range of designs on the market.

♦ Customers do rock backwards on their chairs so choose a robust chair with splayed legs and a strong frame.

- Take a few sample chairs home with you to sit on over several days in your office and your dining room and use constantly to find the most comfortable one.

- Choose chairs that can stack so that you can store them without taking up too much room should the necessity arise or if you have little storage.

- For a more casual, quick turnaround restaurant you still need a chair that is reasonably comfortable and not one that catches you in the backs of the thighs, causing a lot of shifting.

- Most modern ones are wood or a mixture of metal and wood and can make a lot of noise on a wooden floor. Ask the advice of the salesman or manufacturer about how this can be overcome as it can be very distracting for other diners and cause wear and tear on staff's nerves.

- Fixed seating like banquettes are increasingly popular but they are inflexible. Benches in casual restaurants are also gaining in popularity thanks to our increasingly laid-back society.

- As a guide, a chair seat is usually 46 cm from the ground, its depth from the front edge of the seat to the back of the chair also 46 cm. The height from the ground to the top of the back is 1 metre.

Flooring, walls and ceilings

Wooden flooring is *the* chosen flooring for new and revamped restaurants. It looks smart, clean, light and is easy to maintain. The drawbacks are high volume noise levels when chairs are scraped on the floor when diners sit or leave. There is no cushioning of noise – voices, plates, cutlery, music – that could be soaked up by carpeting.

However, carpeting stains, absorbs smell, needs more cleaning and doesn't have the longevity of wooden flooring. It can also deaden noise and therefore lessen the character of a bustling, buzzing place. But, if you have several levels of floor space, you could have some carpet and some wood which accentuates atmosphere.

Wallpaper is out, painted walls are in. Absorbent materials for the ceiling well help enormously in controlling noise. Beware of too low a ceiling which will add to heat and noise. Lighting and electrical points must be designed before decoration.

Consider having heating installed under the floor before laying flooring and ventilation (and air-conditioning too if this is your choice) for reducing smoke and cooking smells before tackling the ceiling.

Toilets

Toilets are often the least concern of many restaurateurs, preferring to spend their money on other aspects of the business. But the British are a finickety lot and are aghast at poorly maintained, shoddy loos and often will cross a restaurant off their list of where to eat out if this is the case.

However, a new breed of toilets is thankfully making its mark in corporate restaurants, other restaurateurs taking note. Smart stand-alone bowls, mixer taps (and not before time!), innovative glass panels, good-sized mirrors, ventilation and subdued, flattering lighting are just some decent design features. It shows a respect for the customer even if the customer doesn't reciprocate in quite the same way.

Some points:

♦ Make sure that the signage to toilets is clear.

♦ Designate staff to keep the toilets clean during opening hours. Nothing is more depressing than to enter toilets strewn with used paper towels, dirty sinks, loo paper on cubicle floors and overflowing bins. Have a weekly rota of staff to carry out checks before each service.

♦ Design the toilets for easy maintenance.

♦ Make sure before service that there is plenty of toilet paper in each cubicle.

♦ If the toilets are small don't install a hand dryer which will heat up the room to uncomfortable levels. Put in paper towels instead or an extending towel roller. Hand dryers add to the noise level too and their efficiency is questionable. How often do you see fellow loo users wiping their hands on their clothes after using a dryer? It's almost the norm.

◆ Make sure all toilet cubicle locks work and are maintained.

◆ If the toilets are close to tables, make sure there is a door to the area that is self-closing. And doesn't squeak.

◆ Do the toilets smell sweet? If not, why not?

◆ Sadly, good toileteries – smart hand soaps, liquid soaps, tissue boxes, cotton wool for makeup removal – disappear. Go for toileteries that are attached to walls, or don't offer anything except soap and towels unless you are in the luxury class and take into budgetary consideration these 'disappearances'.

◆ Do avoid 'funny, ha ha' names like Tou Louse (geddit?) as seen in an arty French eatery, Little Boys and Little Girls rooms and the like.

◆ Keep toilets simple yet smart. But you could go a tad mad with the décor. Add a bit of colour if your restaurant has muted shades.

Lighting

In the showtime analogy of your restaurant offering a sense of theatre, showmanship and pleasure, lighting is one of the most important factors to get right. It adds atmosphere, a warming colour and tone and makes the food even more appealing.

Some tips:

◆ Use dimmers to create instant atmosphere and mood but don't make the restaurant too dark so that reading the menu, a wine list or paying the bill can become a trial rather than a pleasure (the first two at least).

◆ Light fixtures can be as decorative or unobtrusive as suits the décor.

◆ Avoid overhead lighting. It is very harsh. Small inset ceiling lighting can and does work if designed with skill.

◆ Side and uplighting is more flattering than overhead lighting, the women (and even some men) of this world thanking you for this thoughtful, kind lighting.

◆ Table lamps can work in some instances but beware of looking like a lighting showroom with too many table lamps squashed into a small area.

◆ Don't destroy the atmosphere of too bright lighting in halls or coming from the kitchen. Each time the kitchen door opens it lets out a ray of (perhaps) fluorescent light which can kill the mood.

◆ Exterior lighting needs to be welcoming. Light up the mandatory menu frame by the door so that the menu can be easily read by passing trade.

Dressing a table

Table spacing is of great importance, especially in a more formal restaurant. However, a fast, casual restaurant's tables that are close together are more accepted and can add atmosphere.

Table linen

Tablecloths and napkins are expensive to hire and launder. When done in-house without care they can look penny pinching if they are not starched or ironed properly. Cloths suit certain restaurants and not others: a bistro, café or wine bar may not need any. Factor the cost into the day to day expenses of running your restaurant to see if hiring linen is feasible – or not. Get several quotes. Hire companies will also supply glass cloths and hand towels for the toilets.

White or cream is best for showing off food, glasses and flowers and convey a freshness and cleanliness to the restaurant. Dark cloths add a gloom and don't help the food. The materials for dark tablecloths are usually of an inferior type to crisp white or cream linen.

Of course, if your friendly neighbourhood restaurant is better suited to red and white check tablecloths to entice people in and to convey a pleasingly cheap and cheerful place, then follow your instincts. Or you may wish to go down the continental route with paper tablecloths. Or paper tablecloths over a cloth.

Tablecloth sizes:

- 137cm x 137cm to fit a table 76 cm square or 1 metre round table.

- 183 cm x 183 cm to fit a table 1 metre square.

- 183 cm x 244 cm to fit rectangular tables.

- 183 cm x 137 cm to fit smaller rectangular tables.

- Slipcloths (to cover just the top of the tablecloth): 1 m x 1 metre.

- Linen napkins: 46-50 cm square.

- Buffet tablecloths: 2 metres x 4 metres – minimum size.

- Tea and glass cloths: the best are linen or cotton.

Napkins should be simply folded in half. Gone are the days of showing off your staff's origami skills. They have better things to do with their time and skills. Nor should they be picked up and draped over the customer's lap. This is unwarranted affectation and usually an embarrassment to the customer.

Flowers

If dressing your tables with flowers there is no need for an entire bouquet as a single stemmed rose in a simple, clear glass vase will add class and colour. Tall flower arrangements should be avoided as customers may not be able to see one another – not what people come to restaurants for.

Cutlery

When buying cutlery, try it out to see how comfortable it is in your hands. Go for a simple, unfussy design which will not become dated. Buy quality as it won't tarnish. Staff have enough to do without resorting to removing stains from cutlery before setting tables. There is no need for an armed phalanx of cutlery to be placed on the table. Cutlery for one course will do, with added cutlery depending on subsequent ordered courses. Simple is best.

Glasses

Do avoid the temptation of buying glasses for their looks alone as the shape and thinness of a glass can have a marked effect on wine. Thick Paris goblets are a big no-no. They may last forever but don't do anything for wine. Go instead for a plain, clear glass with a good-sized bowl that tapers towards the rim so that customers can swirl the wine around to release the aromas and flavours.

Avoid overly huge balloon glasses which may denote largesse but will easily break and cause your staff to have nervous breakdowns washing and drying them.

Always wash glasses immediately then rinse in hot water and dry. Before setting on tables or putting on shelves re-wipe them with a clean cloth to remove any lurking tinge of detergent, a sure-fire way of ruining wine.

Water glasses and other glasses should be in the same design as wine glasses for continuity and style.

Other items

Ashtrays and condiments should preferably be simply designed to avoid 'walking'. The more covetable the items, the more you will have to replace them. If using the currently trendy salt and pepper mills make sure they are of decent quality, i.e. they do their job properly, or they will need to be replaced at a cost to profits.

Candles are here to stay. Just make them user-friendly, i.e. not tall, precarious ones that can be knocked over or get in the way of service.

Marketing on tables should be considered, depending on your type of restaurant. Have menus, cards, special deals, promotions, events on takeaway cards with some on tables (don't clutter or oversell) and others at strategic points around the restaurant.

THE KITCHEN

The hub of the restaurant has to work efficiently. Restaurants can fail on the basis of a poorly designed kitchen so it is important to consult with a professional if you are new to the restaurant business.

Ask a commercial kitchen equipment company for their advice. You may be taking over a premises that already has some equipment and adding other equipment to upgrade the kitchen.

Or you may be starting from scratch. Do involve the chef, partners in the business, the builder, plumber, carpenter and architect in these crucial discussions, be it an upgrade or a whole new kitchen.

A restaurant kitchen is divided into:

◆ prepping area;

◆ cooking area;

◆ washing up area;

◆ and service.

Storage takes place in all four areas.

A smaller kitchen operation may have to compromise on space while larger kitchens will have the following prepping areas to function at speed:

◆ vegetables;

◆ fish;

◆ poultry;

◆ meat;

◆ desserts.

◆ TOP TIP ◆

Contrary to popular belief, it is not necessary to have a huge kitchen to operate well. A galley kitchen can work excellently for a small restaurant as there is little walking involved and everything is to hand apart from perhaps the storage, fridges and freezer which will be nearby. A further, excellent advantage is that the kitchen is constantly being cleaned up as the chef(s) cook. A good rhythm is established by the chef.

Kitchen needs

The first consideration is what you expect the kitchen to achieve. What kind of food will you be putting on the menu? The menu will dictate what kind of equipment you need and where it should be placed for efficiency and practicality. What can the kitchen handle?

It's not how much a kitchen costs but what you do with it. What is your budget? Will future chefs the proprietor takes on be able to adapt to the kitchen set up by the current chef? Basics like good knives, a solid cooker, large refrigerator and good storage space are prerequisites, so chefs must – and do – adapt.

Consult the *Yellow Pages* for catering companies that supply the large equipment, pots and pans, clothing, knives. Your library will have London and other large towns' *Yellow Pages* (or go on the web) for large specialist companies. Or ask a restaurateur or two for personal recommendations.

Kitchen flow

After deciding on the type of food to emerge the kitchen flow is the next consideration: flow for deliveries to storage spaces, flow of prepared food to service, flow to the dining room and dirty dishes from the dining room, plus flow of waiting staff *vs* kitchen staff in the kitchen. Rarely should they physically meet in the kitchen.

For example, if waiting staff are responsible for the bread, the butter and other peripherals, these must be accessible at some point in the kitchen or service station in the restaurant where they won't stop chefs in their tracks.

Kitchen legislation

Your local environmental health officer should be consulted prior to work on the kitchen to ensure that all necessary steps are taken to abide by legislation. See Chapters 3 and 5 for the role of the EHO, information on ventilation, refuse, water, drainage, pest control, Food Safety Acts, disabled access and safety in the kitchen.

Kitchen equipment

The basic kitchen requirements:

- A double oven with four or six gas burners and a solid top (a solid piece of metal that covers the whole stove, the burner underneath spreading heat all around for keeping items warm or for cooking when turned up).

- A grill or salamander (high level grill).

- A deep fat-fryer.

- A large commercial fridge or walk-in fridge.

- A freezer.

- Double sink.

- Hand basin.

- Sink, preferably near the cooking area.

- Washing up area with commercial dishwasher and storage shelving.

- Hot plate with infra-red lamps if space and money allows (I found it invaluable in my restaurant kitchen) for plating up and situated where waiting staff can easily access it.

- A cool work surface for cold food, pastry and salad prep away from ovens.

- Work surfaces for prepping food and surfaces for food processors, for example.

- Hanging pot and pan racks to increase storage space, preferably by stoves.

◆ Good, accessible storage for cooking equipment, glasses, cutlery, serving dishes, plates etc. Time and motion studies should be worked out: plates near the plating area, coffee cups by the coffee prep area for example.

◆ Rack for food orders placed in order taken.

◆ Good lighting and decent air flow.

◆ A telephone.

If using a microwave, make a space for it. Other equipment to consider: a steamer, a griddle, a convection oven for pastry, a professional ice cream maker, other refrigeration and freezers.

Other spaces are required for:

◆ Cool vegetable and fruit produce storage area away from heat.

◆ Dry goods storage away from heat.

◆ Non-food storage for linen.

◆ Non-food storage for cleaning materials, buckets, mops, light bulbs, toilet paper, refuse bags, vacuum cleaner.

◆ Alcohol storage.

◆ Rubbish.

◆ Office for paperwork. Don't underestimate the amount of paperwork! If no space is available try to find a permanent spot to store it and process the paperwork in the restaurant when closed.

◆ Storage for staff belongings.

Buying equipment

Look for good, solid equipment on castors for easy cleaning and consider second-hand equipment for cutting down the cost of the kitchen. But buy sensibly, not just because it's a bargain. It may not be a few months down the line.

The restaurant you are taking over may have suitable equipment included in the price. If so, make sure all is in working order, establish who services the equipment, get any attached paperwork from the seller of the business and insist that it is cleaned thoroughly before you take over the property.

If buying from specialists, ask for training to be given on the equipment to kitchen staff who should be familiar with most if not all of it, if humanly possible.

◆ TOP TIP ◆

Always have a commercial dishwasher installed. It takes a fraction of the time of a domestic one, the interior is designed without frills to fit in the maximum amount of dishes or pots and pans. There is usually a separate tray for glass washing.

Checklist of cooking equipment to fill those shelves:

- heavy duty cast iron frying pans;
- sauté pans, shallow pans, Dutch ovens (for braising, sauteing or stews);
- pancake pan;
- steamer;
- cast iron casseroles with lids;
- fish pan;
- heavy based stock pots;
- heavy based saucepans for sauces etc;
- knives for many uses – only buy good quality, they will last a lifetime (see Tips on page 89);
- chopping boards (see EHO guidelines);
- plastic lidded containers for food storage and labels;
- mixing bowls of all sizes;
- measuring jugs;

- kitchen scales;

- whisks;

- ladles;

- large spoons;

- slotted spoons;

- kitchen scissors;

- sieves and colanders;

- chinois (fine sieve);

- graters;

- terrines, ramekin dishes;

- roasting and baking trays;

- pastry brushes;

- spatulas;

- lemon squeezer;

- nutmeg grater;

- fish slice;

- pepper and salt mill;

- apple corer;

- funnel;

- corkscrew;

- lemon zester;

- mandoline;

- cheese grater;

- and anything else that is suited to your menu.

Knives

◆ TOP TIP ◆

It never pays to buy cheap knives. Look out for Gustav, Emil & Ern, Sabatier, Sheffield Steel, Victorinox, Ed. Wustof and my favourite, J. A. Henkels.

I still have cherished knives from my 1980s restaurant days which, despite the outlay, are in excellent condition and are as effective as the day they were bought. Chefs will provide their own sets which have been built up over their career.

the basics:

◆ large chopping knife;

◆ sharpening steel or electric/water sharpener;

◆ palette knife;

◆ carving knife;

◆ chef's knife – 15 cm;

◆ medium knife – 20-25 cm;

◆ filleting knife (for fish);

◆ several paring knives (like a vegetable knife);

◆ potato peeler;

◆ meat cleaver;

◆ ham slicer with supple blade;

◆ boning knife;

◆ salmon knife;

◆ bread knife;

◆ cheese knife;

◆ cooking fork.

◆ TOP TIP ◆

High carbon, stainless steel knives won't discolour or rust but will need more sharpening. The sharpest knives are made from carbon steel but can discolour when slicing onions or other acidic food.

If a carbon steel knife is badly discoloured, wet it, sprinkle with kitchen salt and rub vigorously with a cut lemon. A piece of burnt cork is useful for rusty knives.

When buying knives look for balance and weight.

Keep knives on a wall-mounted rack, never in a drawer with other equipment.

Wash and dry knives immediately. Never soak them.

Keep knives sharp at all times. Inexperienced staff using blunt knives can injure themselves.

Look in the *Yellow Pages* for knife sharpeners who do the restaurant kitchen rounds or invest in an electric/water sharpener for in-house sharpening.

CHINA AND TABLEWARE

Depending on the style of the restaurant, the choices are **bone china,** which may be chosen by a no expense-spared restaurant, or **earthenware,** the most popular due to its strength and affordability. **Stoneware,** a natural ceramic durable finish which is more costly than earthenware, may suit a variety of small, casual restaurants.

White or cream tableware shows off food to best advantage and also blends in with every conceivable décor. Patterned china can become dated and tiresome if the design is too busy and it may also be difficult to replace long-term. Your best bet is therefore plain china. But don't see this as limiting, as shapes, sizes and a coloured rim can all add a bit of class and dash if this is what you are seeking.

Do, however, look for durability and rolled edges that can withstand lots of handling and washing. Is the make dishwasher-proof and is there a guarantee from manufacturers that the chosen china will be around for many years to replace broken, chipped or 'gone-walking' items?

If you are choosing super-sized plates, large soup bowls or rectangular shaped plates, do bear in mind the strength of your waiting staff's wrists and the extra miles they may have to walk if only two plates can be carried at one time. Will those varied, angular designs be more prone to chipping? Will fewer be able to fit into your dishwasher at one time, thereby bumping up the cost of cleaning if more washes are made?

A rule of thumb re amounts of china to invest in per restaurant cover:

◆ 4 small plates;

◆ 4 medium sized plates;

◆ 2 large plates;

◆ 2 soup plates or bowls;

◆ 2 cups and saucers;

◆ 4 serving dishes (if plating main courses and serving vegetables or salads separately);

◆ $1\frac{1}{2}$ butter dishes, milk jugs, sugar bowls, tea and coffee pots.

But before investing in china and taking that rule of thumb as gospel consider:

◆ the type of menu on offer;

◆ the maximum and average seating capacity;

◆ the rush hour turn-over;

◆ the washing up facilities and turn-over.

Underplates

For more upmarket restaurants, underplates are still used for improving presentation (or ostentation, depending on your point of view) and for carrying soup plates or bowls. They are also used to ease the carrying of hot items and for carrying cutlery alongside the dish being transferred from one place to another.

Doilies are past their sell-by date but a napkin, paper or otherwise, can help the non-slipping of bowls to get to their destination on an underplate.

Presentation plates are common in Michelin star restaurants and other similarly expensive restaurants to add an extra plushness to the meal. They are often gold-rimmed, strikingly patterned plates which are then whisked away before the customer can even add a fingerprint. The choice is yours but they don't do anything for me and, I suspect, they make the average diner a little uncomfortable and question why they exist at all.

◆ TOP TIP ◆

When storing and stacking china, don't go for the Great Wall of China but instead a mini one of no more than 24 plates to prevent a Great Fall.

Cutlery

Thankfully, the banks of cutlery that can be so off-putting for diners unused to many courses have been mainly phased out, most restaurateurs preferring to keep it simple. No need to buy soup spoons for example, as dessert and soup spoons can perform the same task. Some may, however, disagree. Fork and knife sizes can be the same size so there is no need to buy differing sizes. But you may still need a butter knife which should preferably be small to balance on a side plate. It can double up as a cheese knife too.

In today's eating out society, forget pastry forks, sugar tongs, grapefruit spoons, asparagus holders, curved point cheese knives. They belong, thankfully, in the dainty past.

Stainless steel or silver plate? Which will you choose? Before deciding look at plain patterns and cutlery that will last and not stain. Get a guarantee from the manufacturer re the life span, clean it well and store your cutlery with care to help to prolong its life.

Plainly designed cutlery, like china, will not date and will clean more easily and be more hygienic. But do choose it after selecting your china. It has to complement the china and add to the style of the restaurant.

Stainless steel is available in a variety of grades and is finished by different degrees of polishing: high polish, dull polish and a light matt.

Silver plate has two grades: standard for general use and restaurant thicker grade.

◆ TOP TIP ◆

Store your cutlery in individual drawers or spaces at a convenient height for staff. The use of long, rectangular baskets for a more casual restaurant is quite common. When drying cutlery, place on a tray to remove it to the storage space to reduce handling. Make sure that all cutlery, when placed on tables, is clean and untarnished.

SERVICE

As mentioned previously, it is important to get service right, with flow from the kitchen to the restaurant and vice versa. When waiting staff come in with the order or leave with the food it is preferable that they do so with as little disturbance as possible. So the collection point should be as near to the door as can be achieved.

Where plates and other dirty items will be cleared to also needs to be thought about to achieve a smooth running kitchen and restaurant.

Possible solutions:

◆ Arrange the orders in order of receipt on the check rack and remove when the order has left.

◆ Plated food should be placed on the hot plate under the infra-red lights prior to being taken to the restaurant, so that it can keep warm before staff arrive to deliver the completed dish.

◆ Position stacks of plates on a warmer or in a warming oven in proximity to ovens for plating up – or on a shelf above the warming plate.

◆ Cold food should be removed from refrigeration in good time for it to come close to, or be at, room temperature so that the food actually tastes how it should rather than diminished by the cold.

◆ Cheese is especially poorly served if not brought to room temperature before service.

◆ Position the washing up area and plate clearing so that little overlap goes on and it doesn't encroach on the cooking and prepping area.

◆ From a hygiene point of view it is important that these areas are separate and are designed so that they are kept out of the way of cooking staff.

7

Marketing Your Business

Marketing is one of the most important aspects of your business to get right. It also pays to keep on examining your strategies during the running of your restaurant and to keep re-evaluating your strengths – and weaknesses. As the restaurant market is such a varied one, you need to demonstrate what kind of an establishment you are running so that no mixed messages are sent out. A clear, concise message to potential and existing customers is your goal.

The market is steadily becoming more sophisticated and the numbers of good restaurants to choose from are increasing quite considerably. It therefore isn't enough to sit back and think that your good cooking and beautifully situated, attractive restaurant will pull customers in without some extensive marketing on your part. This is where the first-time restaurateur can become unstuck. **Get a strategy, allocate funding and do your homework.**

◆ TOP TIP ◆

The restaurateur isn't the only salesman. Your front of house staff are equally important to progress your business – and their jobs – so involve them in the process of getting your message across to customers. Get the customers in by marketing and continue the process once they're in. But subtlety is the key for the latter part of the operation. A big sell is a big turnoff.

This chapter covers:

◆ the choosing of a name;

◆ advice on signage to attract customers;

◆ your business cards and stationery;

◆ the menu design

◆ and web pages.

In short, your promotional material.

It also tackles technology via the website, as the internet is increasingly important in marketing – indeed, some say it is vital for survival.

The chapter also discusses the vexed question of advertising and how to launch yourself onto the market. It gives tips on getting a media profile and the importance of getting into the guides that matter.

Constructive advice on dealing with critics, and possible expansion of the business via various routes including cookery classes, corporate lunches and cookbooks is also examined.

A Business Link or Chamber of Commerce in your area may also be useful for assisting you with some of your marketing needs. Costs vary. A well-devised, professionally prepared marketing strategy can be an obvious financial advantage.

FINDING YOUR TARGET MARKET

First you need to identify your initial target market.

1. **Your customers** – age, income, occupations, local businesses.

2. **Your customers' needs** – business lunches, outside catering, Sunday evening openings which may be an untapped market, for example.

3. **The competition** – what attracts customers to other restaurants, what are their strengths, their market share? Is there a reason why there are few restaurants in the area?

4. Trends – changes in local tourism, lifestyle changes, population shifts.

How to get this information:

◆ via the business section of a good, local library;

◆ tourism authorities;

◆ your local Business Link office;

◆ local commerce or traders' groups;

◆ professional market research services;

◆ talk to prospective customers, restaurant staff and suppliers.

CHOOSING YOUR RESTAURANT'S NAME

Do you see your restaurant as a neighbourhood one, a potential crowd-pleaser from afar, a brasserie or bistro, an ethnic restaurant, a gastro pub or café? The name is all-important to attract the type of customer you want to enter your doors.

Choosing a good name for the restaurant is crucial. Avoid gimmicky names at all costs, if you wish to have a reputation as a good restaurant serving quality food and offering good service.

Consider what messages you are sending out with inscrutable, rather questionable names such as Kitch 'n D'Or (oh, yes, it exists), Bizarre Bazaar, Thai Tanic, Cup 'O' Chino and Kwizeen (they do too). I would suggest not very professional ones. It does depend on your market, should you go for a name that incurs a wry smile. Or choose another which fits your aims and personality.

Nor do you wish to choose too bland a name that no one remembers. Or a complicated, tongue-twisting one which a member of staff has to answer the phone to. This vital word-of-mouth marketing tool is also affected if customers can't pronounce the name to pass on to their friends and colleagues.

Obviously choosing a very French or Italian name will pigeonhole you. Potential customers may possibly be put off by the narrow menu it might suggest. Your menu may start off in a French or Italian vein when you open, but if it branches out into Thai, Bangladeshi or fusion cooking of any global kind, passing trade – and customers who haven't been for a while – will not get that broader message. They may walk on, not wishing perhaps to choose from an entirely French or Italian menu, without realising the treasure trove of dishes available.

Equally you may wish to celebrate these types of cuisine, by offering the best of authentic Italian or French food the area has to offer and keeping the menu resolutely to these genres.

Should you be fortunate enough to have a property by a river, capitalise on the location by calling it The Restaurant On The Bridge or equivalent. This does draw people to you who read the guides, write-ups and advertising, always on the lookout for a restaurant with a good view. But call it appropriately and only if there is a view of the water (in this instance). A feeling of being had won't win over new custom. Do avoid clichéd names.

SIGNAGE

Signage, **proper** signage, can have a huge impact on your business if you rely particularly on passing trade or on new customers, having booked, actually finding your restaurant.

- Make first impressions count.

- Never skimp on a professional sign-maker's expertise by making your own signs unless you have the gift.

- Choose an unfussy, readable font to promote your business.

- Match the design and font to your other promotional material.

- Match the sign to your building. If it's modern, do modern. If it's Georgian, avoid going Gothic. Just keep it simple.

- Add the number of the street in lettering large enough to be seen by a passing car.

- Light the signs.

- If you come across a sign in your area which appeals, find out from the business who the sign-maker is in order to contact them.

- If you have a gate, fence or wall by the entry to your premises and use any of these to place your signs on, make sure that bushes and other foliage don't obstruct the signs.

- Consider carefully the colour of the sign and of the lettering for the right impact and legibility. One poorly made sign of dark red with black lettering in my area is illegible; the business has shot itself in the foot before even opening its doors.

- Can your business benefit from several signs for customers approaching from more than one direction?

- Contact your local authority for permission for signage and lighting prior to having the sign made. It may not be passed due to size, colour or lighting so play safe.

- Signage within your business too may be necessary. For professional-ism, it may be advisable to pass on the cutesy 'boys, lads' and 'girls, lasses' room approach which many customers find wince-making.

Contact the local authority for brown tourism signs to which you may be entitled. This signage can have a good effect on your business.

PROMOTIONAL MATERIAL

This includes:

◆ business cards;

◆ printed paper;

◆ flyers;

◆ menus;

◆ sample menus to take away;

◆ newsletter

◆ and web page.

Depending on the type and size of business, you may not want or need all the above promotional material, but some will be obvious essentials. Decide what is necessary for you. A small restaurant may only need business cards, and make their own menus and headed paper via a computer. Or a menu board, clearly written, may be your choice.

Go through fonts very carefully as your choice will demonstrate your professionalism. A funky, angular one will merely be difficult to read. A clean, clear one will show respect for business and customer alike. Choose the same font for all promotional material.

Business cards

Put information on business cards such as restaurant name (it has been seen to be omitted), address, complete telephone number, website (if applicable), days of openings and times, perhaps bullet points of strengths (fresh local fish, sea views, log fires, in the *Good Food Guide*) plus a map on the back if your location is challenging. Will you have a logo?

Keep it simple yet as informative as possible. Make your business cards stand out via design and perhaps colour.

Stationery

Printed paper needs a heading, registered office (if applicable), address, telephone/fax, email, website and logo.

Compliment slips are useful for sending menus or confirmation of a booking or other information by post. Position the 'with compliments' so that you are not forced to write all around it.

Publicity

Flyers

Flyers are useful for leaving information at various sites, for handing out and for passers-by to take away with them. Have all the relevant information (where, what, when open) plus a sample menu and bullet points of strengths (see business cards) on the flyers. They can be A5 or compliment slip size.

Brochures

Brochures are increasingly being used as a market tool by more upmarket restaurants. Add photographs, sample menus and information with opening times, a map and perhaps private dining facilities, car park facilities, outside dining or bar area. A big 'don't do' in my book is photography of smiling people, usually models, who look like the cat's pyjamas as they gaze at one another over a perfectly groomed table awash with lobster tails and stemmed glasses, but not like real people really enjoying themselves at *your* restaurant. Of course you wish your restaurant to look its best, but you don't wish to alienate people by inferring only 'perfect' people or a younger crowd eat here.

Newsletters

Newsletters can be an invaluable help to the small restaurant, keeping regular customers informed of local and calendar events with suggestions of menus to match the event or time of year. Or they may describe a special menu that ties in with a tight schedule, menu changes, new produce, a range of wines new to the list, a celebration of the first year of opening. They can be as personal or restrained as befits your market and can keep your business in your customers' thoughts. Results often come from a mail out.

Menus

Menus are best kept simple, with the name of the restaurant as a heading. Options include printed ones if the menu varies little or seasonally, or clearly hand-written or computer-printed ones if the menu is small and changing daily.

Thanks to computing skills, it is easy to create your menus and print them off on a when-needed basis. Do check menus constantly and discard those that are at all marked. Covers for menus or wine lists must also be kept scrupulously clean and unmarked. A messy menu gives out the wrong impression immediately and may indicate a less than sparkling kitchen.

Sample menus are an excellent marketing device. Don't forget to put the name of the restaurant and other relevant information on these slips. Have these, flyers and business cards, accessible and replenish the space taken up by these marketing tools regularly. As a compulsive collector of menus and flyers I am surprised that these details – name, address, number, website (if appropriate), times of opening – are often omitted, the information therefore useless.

The internet

A website is a boon for business. It is relatively cheap and good for small businesses which have a minimal marketing budget. Research other people's websites and either design yours yourself or choose a designer whose work appeals to you. Ask about the success of the designer's work, i.e. how many hits the website attracts. Look at a variety of websites for design inspiration. Get several quotes before committing yourself. Choose the background colour with care so that the website is readable. Some designers can be too ambitious or funky, and irritating to read so the customer gives up.

For simplicity, have the relevant information on the website, including times and days of opening, how to book a table, sample menu and wine list, a map, a good photograph of the restaurant's exterior (if it merits it) and of the interior. For bigger players, a virtual 360 degree view of the restaurant and other public areas can be a real bonus.

Keep the website updated and either do the upkeep yourself or agree on a monthly/retainer fee with the web designer. Above all, keep it simple and easily navigable. A static website, i.e. one which doesn't change or update, can send out the wrong signals and can arguably be worse than no website at all as it may demonstrate a slack approach. Don't do as some restaurateurs do to make themselves look up to date and add a website address to their promotional material, which, when you visit it, contains nothing. This gives off bad signals.

◆ TOP TIP ◆

Put yourself in the shoes of the potential customer. Check that your website is welcoming, practical, professional looking and geared towards the customers who you would like to attract.

Customers are increasingly looking to the internet for information. In 2003, an estimated 42 per cent of UK households used the internet, making the necessity of tapping into this market self-explanatory. The traffic to your site is dependent on not only the website address on your promotional materials, but also on search engines which will make your marketing endeavours even more productive. Searchers will either have your website address or may key in one specific word or group of words such as 'restaurants in Norwich'.

ADVERTISING

To advertise or not to advertise, that is the question. Look through your local papers and you will see the same restaurants' ads. In my area these are generally ethnic restaurants or ones belonging to chains that can afford the luxury of advertising.

Christmas, Mothering Sunday and Bank Holidays bring out a rash of ads too, from low to middle range or chain restaurants, rarely from those who aim to offer top quality food and service. These ads tend to offer meal deals, the menus often identical, with kids' food at vastly reduced prices.

In my experience as a restaurateur of a small, independent upmarket country restaurant, it simply doesn't pay to advertise. It is far more effective to use other marketing skills to get your message across: via *Yellow Pages*, media relationships, guide books, mail shots, a newsletter, handouts, website, internet, local tourism publications. Word of mouth is one of your most effective marketing tools. It has been estimated that every one satisfied customer will in turn tell between five and ten people.

Targetting the audience

Should you decide to advertise, look carefully at the many local newspapers to see if you are targetting the right audience. Most local newspapers have sister publications more suited to your area. You can obtain a media blueprint from your local publications which will give you a lot of research information. But make sure it is up to date. Look at the website www.jicreg.co.uk (Joint Industry Committee for Regional Press Research) to gauge the readership statistics of the majority of UK newspapers.

When contacting the advertising department ask pertinent questions about:

♦ The circulation.

♦ The readership: age groups, for example, and standard socio-economic categories:

   − A = higher managerial, administrative or professional;

   − B = intermediate managerial, administrative or professional;

   − C1 = junior managerial, administrative or professional;

   − C2 = skilled manual workers;

   − D = semi and unskilled manual workers;

   − E = those at the lowest level of subsistence.

♦ Shopping patterns: taking holidays abroad, buying new cars etc.

♦ Paid or free papers.

♦ The best day to place an ad if a daily paper. Your ad might well be best placed on the entertainment page, for example, which only comes out on Thursdays.

♦ The best section. Always stipulate where you would like your ad and if it appears in an inappropriate page, ask for it to be reprinted at no charge.

See a copy of your ad beforehand to agree it and proof-read it thoroughly. Also look at local magazines and ask the same questions.

Other ways of advertising

These include paid for and free:

♦ *Yellow Pages.*

♦ Posters.

♦ Local tourism publications.

♦ Local Tourist Information offices or Visitor Information Service websites which may have an eating out list.

♦ Direct mail.

♦ Newsletters for promotions, seasonal information, menus, staff changes.

♦ Internet (look at your area for online restaurant sites).

Advertorials

A mix of public relations and ads takes you down a contract route with the paper you choose. The deal is this. You agree to advertise a set number of ads of determinate size, or at least a quarter page ad, and for this you get a glowing report of your restaurant written by you and the advertising department. You will be persuaded to take a series of ads out, the argument being that it isn't worth your while having just one.

The advertorial may include a visit by a staff member for a meal at your restaurant. The style of the place, virtually the entire menu, wine list and character of mine host will be given a 100 per cent thumbs up. This frankly fools no one and is seen as a very cheesy way of going about business. Best avoided if you are aiming at a good, discerning clientele who may run a mile.

Advertising nationally/internationally

Consider advertising in appropriate magazines. Try specialist interest magazines if, for example, your restaurant is in an area of outstanding natural beauty, a boating area, walking, hill-climbing areas or an architecturally stunning city.

Go to your local library and look up the following publication guides:

◆ *Willings*;

◆ *Benn's Media Guide*;

◆ *BRAD (British Rate and Data)*.

These will guide you to what publications are on the market, their approximate advertising costs and how to contact them.

Other possibilities may be to place ads in brochures and programmes allied to sporting events, such as Glorious Goodwood in Sussex, and their associated seasonal events. You are looking for a cut in this lucrative world.

Go to your local Tourist Information office to research brochures and programmes for festivals, theatres, art galleries, art house cinemas and the like to gauge advertising possibilities and their merits.

Advertising wording

Your advertisement is selling your business so it must:

◆ Grab the reader's attention.

◆ Stimulate interest.

◆ Plant the idea firmly in the head of the reader that this may be the place for them and that they should react promptly.

◆ Be concise and give out the appropriate information – who you are, where you are, what you are offering, how you can be contacted, why they should book and when you are open.

◆ If your restaurant is in the *Good Food Guide* or any of the better guides, put this information in your ad.

Don'ts:

◆ Don't be pushy, arrogant or personal.

◆ Don't brag.

◆ Don't use flowery language.

◆ Don't contravene the Trades Descriptions Act by offering something you can't deliver.

Other advertising tips

If you have taken over someone else's business there may be an existing advertising contract. Do re-evaluate this.

When people book, ask them how they heard about your restaurant and compile this information to help you gauge the effectiveness of advertising – or is it a word of mouth booking?

Don't knee-jerk react to a cold call from a sales person offering advertising. They will always try to persuade you with a must-have special offer or deal. Either ignore the call as politely as possible or ask them to send you details and then check the publication to see if the expense is worthwhile.

Do stick to your budget.

Other marketing tips

If you plan to offer a discounted or good value lunch, target retirement establishments and sheltered housing. Distribute or leave menus and flyers in lobbies if permitted, or in lobbies of community centres and other simi-lar places that the retired may be more likely to visit. Lunch is a booming part of business as more and more retired people prefer to lunch and drive/walk home in daylight.

Leave a slip of paper on tables for recruiting names and addresses from customers. Or enclose it with the bill so that you can remind them of your existence via a mail shot of a new menu or a newsletter, updating your cus-tomers about special events.

Make sure you put your restaurant's phone number and address in the *Yellow Pages* and in the telephone directory. You can, of course, put an ad in the *Yellow Pages* too.

THE MEDIA PROFILE

Before you can decide how to attract the media you must first recognise your unique strengths and what you are offering the public – and the media who you would like to woo. Consider what your style is. Is it purely culinary? Mainly looks? Based just on the character of the owner and/or chef? Ideally it's a mix of all three. An independent restaurateur must find his or her own voice, own style to project, to sell to the media.

Free advertising – for this is what you will achieve by having a media pres-ence – must be convincing, otherwise you are treading on dangerous ground when being visited by the guides and critics. If it is all hype and no substance, the damage to your business can be substantial by a bad review.

Before toting for new business via media coverage, you must believe in yourself and be committed to being able to offer what you say you can. Can you deliver the goods? Think about what makes you unique and makes people want to come through your door. It is almost like a unique blueprint fingerprint: no one does it quite like you do, hence the popularity of your restaurant.

Don't latch on to other people's style. You should be true to yourself, other-wise your restaurant may look self-conscious, out of synch, out of place.

Media coverage: who to target

◆ local and national media;

◆ restaurant reviewers, local and national;

◆ restaurant guides.

How to achieve media coverage

Achieve media coverage via personalities who work for you and what is special about your restaurant:

◆ A high-profile chef just taken on or one with an interesting pedigree or background.

◆ A sommelier who knows his or her business and who has worked in a high-profile place, or has an unusual background.

◆ Your produce – perhaps it's unusual or sourced via an unusual producer.

◆ Your building if historic, renovated to a high standard, or on an interesting site.

◆ If you have changed from being a commercial city high-flyer, or nun, or are the first Alaskan to open a restaurant in the area.

◆ Has your restaurant changed hands after a 20 year or so period in the hands of a much-loved, local personality, for example?

This is all newsworthy.

Research

Research your area's newspapers, magazines, radio and television at your local library. Ask for help via your librarian about the publications available. Also, consider reading/buying *The Guardian Media Guide*, and looking up publications in those useful guides, *Willings* and *Benn's*.

Compile a media list of local and national newspapers, magazines, local and national radio programmes, and trade magazines, with contact numbers and emails.

When writing to a newspaper or magazine, phone to find out who to contact first. Write down the correct spelling of their name and send them a press release (see below on how to write one) with a photograph of the interior, the chef, a dish, the new owner. A picture tells a thousand words. But only if your budget can stand the cost of such an exercise. It is a waste of time and money if you don't find out exactly who to target as your press release will simply be tossed out and not forwarded to the right person.

To call or not to call after sending a press release. Journalists are incredibly busy and some find it a distinct irritant to be called. Others don't. It's a gamble and if you do decide to throw caution to the wind, call them within a week or ten days of sending the release to establish first-hand contact.

◆ TOP TIP ◆

Contact radio programme presenters (those who do interviews or have a magazine-style programme) to see if you can be interviewed, again having sent a press release and some background to your business to spark an interest.

It pays to keep your media list up to date and to talk or send a press release on a regular basis to keep you in their focus. But not with non-newsworthy items as they will go straight in the bin – or, worse still, you will be seen as a nuisance. Keep it professional, short and newsworthy.

Press releases

Press releases can be an excellent tool for business promotion if they are properly written and presented. They are not a page-long ad, nor are they a novel. Neither are they a promotional piece full of detail.

One common error is not to have read the publication you are targeting before sending the press release. Do some homework and visit their website and look at the style, the content and, if possible, buy the publication. As a result of your study, you will be able to understand the readers' needs and get a better response from your press release.

Golden rules of writing press releases:

- Use headed paper with contact name, address, phone, email.

- The date of the press release should be prominently displayed.

- State Press Release at the top of the release.

- Write *For Immediate Publication* or *Embargoed to July xx* (if there is a reason for keeping the news until a later date) also at the top.

- Use double-spacing or small paragraphs divided by a space.

- Keep it short: one page, the length between 400–500 words.

- Use one side only of the paper if you must go onto another page.

- Always finish with ENDS.

- Choose your font carefully. It must be easily readable and not quirky.

- Write with the journalist in mind. They are not looking to buy your product or service but to fill a news need.

- Write a press release asking the question: 'Why should readers of *XYZ* care' rather than 'What's in it for me?'

- Start with an underlined heading encapsulating your reasons for sending this press release: e.g.

  Tom Glanville, award-winning chef from The Savoy to join The Dining Room, Bristol, as head chef.

- Develop the press release with newsworthy items, such as what strengths Tom will bring to the restaurant due to his culinary style and background. Tom may be hosting a sample menu tasting or he may be holding a charity promotion or offering cookery courses.

- Finally, add other details at the end, i.e. Notes for editor: The Dining Room, owned and run by Jessica Yates, opened in 1999, is in the *Good Food Guide* and has two rosettes in the *AA Guide*. For further information and for photography contact Jessica Yates – with full contact details.

- Re-read your press release for grammatical errors and spelling mistakes.

- Send the press release by post. If sending via email it may just be ignored or deleted.

CRITICS

Don't confuse advertorials with critics. The former is part of the advertising process with a staff member of the newspaper writing a glowing report of your restaurant. The latter is an unsolicited reviewer of your restaurant who will come unannounced and unbidden.

If you believe in your restaurant then you will welcome a critic, but only one who understands the restaurant business, rather than a celebrity reviewer who may be simply out for him or herself with little knowledge, understanding or interest. These reviewers are usually attention-seeking and have little respect within the restaurant industry. Restaurants generally deserve much better than the reviews these people give.

Critics can be vicious but can equally heap praise on where praise is due. I have been a restaurant critic and restaurant inspector for a number of years and, beforehand, chef and restaurant owner.

Not all critics need to have this background, of course, but it is immensely useful to have been steeped in the business before taking up the critical pen. There are critics who rightly see it from the point of view of the restaurant diner and recognise a restaurant which is giving a raw deal to its customers – or the exact opposite.

Some restaurateurs grumble – after a poor review – that the critic is not an ordinary customer. Granted, there are critics who set preposterous standards of excellence when reviewing a restaurant which has no pretensions, the establishment preferring to offer simpler fare in less ostentatious surroundings. He or she is not doing their job fairly or properly.

What critics look for

Criticism must be based on the food, sourcing of produce, the kitchen's skills, front of house staff, the degree of care and attention shown to the customer and the degree of comfort (at least a decent chair to sit on rather than one that cuts into the backs of your legs).

It is not purely the food the critic has to focus on, however, but also the feel of the restaurant and if the experience was a successful, enjoyable one. Is hospitality offered? Creativity? Innovation? Maybe a theatrical buzz?

Criticism is useless unless the writer can give reasons as to why the food, atmosphere or service was poor. It is simply not good enough to say, 'I didn't like my pork belly with pak choi.' Why not? Was it tough, too salty, the meat poorly sourced, the vegetable wildly overcooked? A critic owes it to the restaurant to explain why.

Critics do have the power to close a business. Their judgement can be that tough on businesses – the ultimate *coup de grace*. I derive no pleasure from it. But some restaurateurs are simply not cut out to be in the business and do unutterable damage to the reputation of the industry. Time to pack up and find another, more fulfilling, suitable profession rather than foisting poor food and service on the public.

Responding to reviews

On the positive side, a good critique of a restaurant can create boom time, the phone ringing non-stop for bookings. If this happens to you, give the critic a call or write. It is always appreciated.

◆ TOP TIP ◆

What if you do get a bad review? Ultimately, your customers are your best critics but if there is a shift down in numbers coming through your door it may be time to reappraise your efforts. If a review was bad and you respect the writer for their style, understanding and fair points, then you must take it on board and resolve to address the criticism.

There will always be times in the life of a restaurant when not everything runs smoothly: your chef burns a hand, a staff member hasn't removed the lipstick from a just-washed glass, late produce delivery means too little time to prep properly. You will just have to accept the negative press reaction should the critic be in that evening. But it is simply no good relying on 'chef's night off' as an excuse. If the chef was off, the deputy has to achieve the same standards. Or close the restaurant that day/evening.

But, if your restaurant has little in the way of commendation and is purely PR hype without substance and you get a real roasting, then it's time to re-evaluate your goals.

National critics respected by most restaurateurs and the public alike include Fay Maschler (*London Evening Standard*) and Jay Rayner (*Observer*). They know their onions and can deliver some pretty savage blows as well as praise when it's due. The ones not to take seriously include Michael Winner (*Sunday Times*). Be very wary of approaching AA Gill (*Sunday Times*) and Victor Lewis-Smith (*Guardian*). They are the rottweilers of the business and have declared open season, seeing restaurants and chefs as personal fair game.

Approaching critics

If you do approach any restaurant critic with information about your restaurant in the hope that you will get a write-up, make sure you do so with your eyes wide open. It is a long shot that your restaurant will be chosen for a write-up by national papers, however. Many of these critics stay firmly in town, only venturing outside London occasionally during their 52 or less weeks of the year's reviewing.

However, regional newspapers that have such a column welcome any reports of a new restaurant opening or change of chef and, if they are worth their salt, will do an anonymous write-up rather than accept an invitation to be your guest. I am always very pleased to know of changes in my area of Hampshire and West Sussex and will put names on my list of restaurants to review. But I will never go as a guest as it could be seen as compromising my objectivity.

THE GUIDES

Why aspire to have an entry in the guides? Depending on which guide you are in – preferably a non fee-paying one – it will add extra publicity and respect. The reader will seek out the best one suited to their needs in their own area or in other areas of the country they intend visiting for pleasure or work. But there are good, mediocre and bad guides. I simply list the ones that matter in the trade, the ones that restaurateurs aspire to achieve an entry in rather than the guides in which you pay to have an entry. Your customers are, generally speaking, a discerning lot and can sniff an advertising puff when they come across it.

Les Routiers is a case in point. The famous blue and red symbol, since its inception in 1935 in France, indicates hotels and restaurants of individual character. They are often managed by the owner and offer 'good food, warm hospitality and excellent value for money.'

And in the twenty-first century? These are still the guiding principles, according to Nicholas Stanley, Managing Director. Les Routiers Limited is a network of independent restaurants, pubs and hotels located in the UK and Ireland but is also an 'umbrella organisation marking their shared values and individual appeal through the Les Routiers brand.' In short, you pay for the privilege and submit your own copy. Small restaurants are from £450, establishments with over 50 covers £600 for their marketing membership.

I wouldn't wish anyone to spend a penny in some restaurants in the guide which I have reviewed as a restaurant critic. Not only has the food been bad but the service and establishment too. Paradoxically it also lists some very good restaurants, management having taken the decision to spread their restaurant's publicity wings widely by having an entry in the guide. The choice, of course, is theirs and yours. If you wish to find out more about entry contact info@routiers.co.uk.

Top guides, as recognised by restaurateurs and customers, are without doubt *The Good Food Guide* and *The Michelin Guide* in the UK and Ireland. Other good guides include *The AA Restaurant Guide*, *Harden's UK Restaurants* (although not a favourite of many restaurateurs), *Time Out Eating and Drinking in Great Britain and Ireland*, *Time Out Eating and Drinking In London* and Georgina Campbell's *Jameson Guide Ireland*. *The Zagat Survey* can also be useful.

◆ TOP TIP ◆

Do submit your restaurant to guides with details, menu, wine list, how to find you and a covering letter in the hope that an inspector may come calling.

The AA Restaurant Guide

This hefty tome, nearly 700 pages in 2004, lists 675 stand-alone restaurants and 1,200 restaurants that are part of hotels. The AA has a mere 30 inspectors and awards AA rosettes. These go from one rosette for 'excellent local restaurants serving food prepared with care, understanding and skill, using good quality ingredients' to five rosettes, awarded to 'the finest restaurants in the British Isles, where cooking stands comparison with the best in the world.' Four restaurants achieved this accolade in the 2004 guide.

AA rosettes are awarded solely for the cooking and consistency, the standard to be achieved 'regardless of the chef's day off!' Ambience, style, comfort, layout and presentation of menu, appearance, attitude and efficiency of service and the quality of the wine list 'should all fit the ambition of the cooking' too. There are other entries too for non-rosette winners.

My quibble with the guide is its layout, with very busy pages and some inconsistencies making it a bit of a challenge to negotiate and read. All that text, all those pictures, all those counties crashing into one another with nary a gap. Are the inspectors discriminating enough? There are some entries I would not have put in the guide but this is subjective. It is out of date too, with a number of restaurants that closed way before the guide was printed. Maps are not easy on the eye either.

There is no payment required for entry but pictures cost. The editor welcomes restaurants to submit their details for inspection and, hopefully, inclusion.

The AA Restaurant Guide has a competition, the AA Chefs' Chef, an annual poll of all the chefs in the guide who vote to recognise the achievements of one of their peers from a shortlist. Michel Roux of the Waterside Inn, Bray, was the 2004 winner.

Website: www.theaa.com

Georgina Campbell's *Jameson Guide – Ireland's best places to eat, drink and stay*

Georgina Campbell, indefatigable writer on Irish cuisine and hospitality, conceived this guide in 1998, its main sponsor being Jameson Irish Whiskey.

It covers over 900 restaurants, pubs, country houses, hotels, cafés, guest-houses and farmhouses throughout the north and south of Ireland, and prides itself on highlighting the quality and the variety of Irish produce.

It is particularly interested in restaurants giving the provenance of their ingredients on menus, with the emphasis on quality from artisan producers.

The no-gimmick verbose guide, written with heart-and-soul, has a rating system with a quirky demi-star denoting a restaurant approaching full-star status. Three stars is the highest rating. It rightly celebrates the culinary revolution that has taken place in Ireland over the past 20 years.

There is a sister guide, Georgina Campbell's *Jameson Guide Dublin* which lists restaurants by post code (as does the main guide in the capital) and by cuisine and speciality. Both assess entries independently and there is no payment for inclusion. No advertising is allowed by entries.

Website: www.ireland-guide.com

The Good Food Guide

The Good Food Guide was first published in 1952, then taken up and published by the *Which? Consumers Guides* in 1962. It is the one found in keen diners' cars for searching for a recommended restaurant en route in town or country, with perhaps another copy at home for research or simply drooling over the descriptions of the food and places.

The unmistakable initials – *GFG* – are part of its unmistakable character. The idea to promote and find good food came about after World War Two as a club for those consumers unable to stand another plate of beige food and who wished to put quality back into meals.

Raymond Postgate, the first editor, created the first stocky little pocket edition in those post-war years. Inspectors recruited over 50 years included a future Chancellor of the Exchequer, three world-famous English conductors, a socialist bishop and John Arlott, the cricket commentator.

In those first editions you could also find a 1934 Chambertin for 18 shillings, dinner at the Lygon Arms for 18/6d and, sociologically, a fascinating study of past indignities including one of women, by order of management, forbidden to be served at the bar. This notice was prominently displayed in a Castle Combe hotel and would have been wrenched from its site by subsequent generations of both men and women.

The *GFG* continues to be very much a compendium of shared experiences by readers and inspectors. Andrew Turvil is the guide's sixth and current editor and his illustrious predecessors have included Christopher Driver, Drew Smith, Tom Jaine and Jim Ainsworth.

This shared wealth of knowledge covers 1,000 main entries and 300 in a round-up section of the best on offer in England, Wales, Scotland, Northern Ireland, the Republic of Ireland and the Channel Islands.

'We look for restaurants serving fresh food carefully prepared, as simple as that,' according to Andrew, 'and it can include anything from a small café serving perfectly fresh unadorned seafood to a smart restaurant delivering the finest *haute cuisine*. If it's enjoyed by our readers and approved by inspectors, it will appear in the *GFG*.'

How the GFG works

There are currently 70 inspectors nationally and they are the eyes and ears on the ground, to say nothing of the taste buds being given quite a workout. They are freelance, keep the guide informed of what's going on in their area and undertake official yet anonymous visits on behalf of the guide.

Some have professional experience in the hospitality industry as either chefs or restaurateurs, others are food and wine journalists and the rest are readers of the guide.

Each inspection is undertaken as a full meal, usually for two people so that the experience is the same as for a typical diner.

There have been a few changes over the years since my restaurant's entries in the guide. The cooking marks are now from one to ten rather than up to five, giving it more scope for definition of requirements. It also has a new font and page format, but the original ethos is still there. A very readable, unfussy, user-friendly guide with easy to follow symbols and good layout. Published yearly in September.

Restaurants are not charged for inclusion in the guide. Contact the guide to let them know you exist, send in menus, wine list and information about your restaurant and staff and hopefully an inspection will follow. Good Food Guide, 2 Marylebone Road, London NW1 4DF.

Website: www.which.net *Good Food Guide*

Harden's UK Restaurants

One of the simpler, easier to read guides on the market 'where real people eat'. It includes restaurants, country house hotels, pubs, curry houses and chippies – and 'pulls no punches', according to its editors.

Published in October each year, *Harden's* relies on a comprehensive survey of regular restaurant goers and analyses around 80,000 reports on 1,500 restaurants, including ones in Dublin.

Categories on the survey include 'top gastronomic experience', 'your favourite restaurant', 'best bar/pub food', 'most romantic', 'most disappointing cooking' and several other ethnic and cuisine categories. Their rating is one to five (one being excellent, five being disappointing).

Remy Martin, sponsors of the guide, award Restaurant Remys to new and up and coming restaurants, with ten each in London and outside the capital.

No fee is payable for inclusion in this guide or its sister guide, *Harden's London Restaurants* (published in September), nor is any advertising or hospitality accepted.

In London, all 1,200 restaurants are visited by its editors. The UK restaurants are inspected only if they are notably interesting. All editors' visits are paid for by the guide.

Also included in both guides are forthcoming openings of note with a brief, non-critical entry outlining contact details. The deadline for submissions is early July for the London restaurants and early August for UK ones.

Harden's Guides were conceived in 1992 (the London guide) and 1998 (UK guide) by brothers Richard and Peter Harden, and have 'an enviable knack of getting the verdict right in as few words as possible' says *Scotland On Sunday's* restaurant critic. The *Irish Times* goes one better: 'Utterly and ruthlessly honest.' But, as mentioned in the introduction to the guides, a number of restaurateurs have an aversion to this one.

Website: www.hardens.com

The Michelin Guide

The Michelin Guide, conceived in France in 1900 for hungry motorists, now has eight guides covering 21 European countries. The UK one was first published in 1974. It covers hotels and restaurants with minimal wording, its timeless symbols denoting facilities, features and categories.

The guide, published annually, employs only 70 full-time inspectors, who have training and experience in the hotel and catering industry for the whole of Europe. Each establishment 'is visited and/or tested by our staff at least once in the year', including many that don't make the grade.

This is the guide many chefs aspire to, a Michelin star adding huge kudos firstly to the chef, the restaurant taking second place. If the chef decamps, the star is lost to both chef and restaurant.

Three Michelin stars: 'Exceptional cuisine, worth a special journey – one always eats here extremely well, sometimes superbly. Fine wines, faultless service, elegant surroundings. One will pay accordingly.'

Two Michelin stars: 'Excellent cooking, worth a detour – specialities and wines of first class quality. This will be reflected in the price.'

One Michelin star: 'A very good restaurant in its category – the star indicates a good place to stop on your journey. But beware of comparing the star given to an expensive 'de luxe' establishment to that of a simple restaurant where you can appreciate fine cooking at a reasonable price.'

Other restaurant symbols include crossed knives and forks – one to five – which denote the degree of comfort, the latest addition being a fork and mug for traditional pubs serving good food.

The Bib Gourmand, with the Michelin man's head in red, denotes good food at moderate prices (£25) at a less elaborate restaurant.

In the UK 2004 guide only three places were awarded three Michelin stars, with 11 two-stars, 96 one-stars and some 5,621 restaurants awarded entry.

Michelin updates

In the past, it was perceived that, in order to gain a star, lavish comfort was one irrefutable necessity. This has been relaxed quite considerably due to changing, more informal times. Two pubs have been awarded stars in the latest guide, unthinkable only a few years ago.

A Michelin inspector (now ex) recently wrote a controversial book about the guide, stating that the gourmet restaurant bible was understaffed, out of date and in thrall to big-name chefs in France. A number of restaurateurs and critics were not taken aback by these criticisms as they had felt the guide had lost some of its authority. Despite this, it is still seen by many as a true reflection of good restaurants (and hotels) in the 21 countries featured in the eight published guides. Inclusion is free. The *UK Guide* is published in mid-January. Website www.themichelinguide-gbirl@uk.michelin.com

Time Out Eating and Drinking in Great Britain and Ireland and *The Time Out London Eating and Drinking Guide*

The London guide, first published in 1983, was followed by the Great Britain and Ireland one in 2004, with 1,200 entries in each well-produced, independent publication. These are the books that are the most helpful and readable and come from the large *Time Out* stable of guides.

London Guide

In the London guide, restaurants are considerately grouped into types and ethnicity (brasserie, pubs, wine bars, Greek, Italian, Thai, for example), eating on a budget and by area. There is also a useful list of where to do brunch, Sunday lunch, late eating, eating alone, taking a date, taking the kids, spotting a celeb, finding the unfamiliar and loving the look. Innovative.

It includes too a list of new restaurants and closures, immensely good boxed information giving the lowdown on Sri Lankan, Thai, Indian food etc, with explanations of words and dishes you may find on menus.

A red star denotes a very good restaurant of its type, a green star helping to identify a more budget conscious eatery. Annual awards are given for best bar, pub, local restaurant, gastropub, family restaurant, Indian restaurant, cheap eat, vegetarian meal, design, new restaurant and an award for outstanding achievement. Excellent photography too.

Ireland Guide

The Time Out Eating and Drinking in Great Britain and Ireland, a small volume in comparison, is a very welcome addition to the national scene and uses the same star system and other helpful information. Regional listing includes London but I do question why some of the entries in both volumes have been included and others left out.

Around 50 'mostly' freelance inspectors, mainly food journalists, are their writers. Good, clear maps in both guides. No payment to be included in either book. 'Places are re-reviewed each year.'

Website: www.timeout.com

The Zagat Survey

Started by New Yorkers Tim and Nina Zagat in 1979 there has been a *London Restaurant Guide* for years. It is just one of the many guides in the US and Europe to have emerged via the Survey which invites diners to rate and review restaurants and many other leisure pursuits they have visited.

However, this quirky read can become tiresome. It does have a location index, useful 'all day dining', 'breakfast/brunch' and many more categories to look up. Not always up to date and not widely known except for aficionados of the genre. Website: www.zagat.com

Local lists

Your local tourist information office may have a list of restaurants to which you can add your premises. Also scout around the web to link your restaurant to your area. There may also be other websites you can be part of.

Do contact the local media via a press release if you are entered in a prestigious guide (see how to write a press release). Contact the national media if you have been awarded a Michelin star, an AA rosette or are given a high rating in *The Good Food Guide*.

BUSINESS EXPANSION

There are slack times in the restaurant trade, be they seasonal or due to geography. Think therefore of adding some extra strings to your bow like cookery classes, outside catering, takeaway, writing for a local or national magazine or newspaper, or targetting the corporate market with special lunch deals.

Loyalty cards and comment cards

If you are going down the fast, casual restaurant route think of a loyalty or privilege card that many corporate coffee businesses like Caffe Nero offer. The card accumulates points against future purchases with x number of points for a free coffee, xxx points for a meal for two.

Comment cards are good for market research, the card's tick boxes including name and address of customer and/or email address, cleanliness, service, food enjoyment, welcome etc with a few lines for customers' comments.

Cookery classes

When is your least busy period? Just after Christmas? The dark days of autumn or winter? If you are a communicator why not capitalise on your premises and your profession to create a series of cookery classes and/or demonstrations. These can be instead of a lunch trade one day (choose a slack day) every month or if the restaurant has a weekly closing day.

Write to your customers via a newsletter, put up posters and distribute flyers in the restaurant, in libraries, shops and elsewhere in your area. Outline a daily, weekly or monthly set of classes for six or more paying students (it generally won't pay to have less) depending on your kitchen size.

Design the classes carefully around your own prep time, leaving plenty of time to clear up, have some time off and prepare for the evening.

◆ TOP TIP ◆

Plan the cooking with a domestic kitchen in mind and don't use hard to find ingredients. Don't be too technically advanced or you may lose your students. Do have a member of staff in to wash up during the class, and help prep before the students' arrival, and put this cost into your budget.

Possible timetable no 1: 9.30 am arrive: coffee and talk. 10 am: start students cooking a two-course meal (or whatever you have chosen to do). 12.30: lunch with a glass of wine in restaurant. 2 pm: discussion of cooking and questions and answers. Departure: 3.30 pm with pack containing recipes, restaurant menus, public relations information.

Possible timetable no 2: 10 am: arrival and coffee. Demonstration: 11 am–12.30 pm. Glass of wine with food cooked either still in kitchen or informally in the restaurant. Leave 1.30 with tips and recipe pack plus menu and PR.

Offer gift vouchers for classes and demonstrations.

Types of classes

Daily, two to three day course, weekly, occasional or seasonal. You could teach:

- The basics: soups, breads, patés, roasts, simple desserts, jams, biscuits.

- Cooking for family and friends: simple oven dishes using chicken or pasta.

- Cooking lunch with your paying cooks from scratch and eating the meal in the restaurant with a good glass of wine.

- Food from Morocco, Spain, Italy, France, Thailand, Mexico, each country covered in a series of hands-on cooking classes or demonstrations.

- Cooking with spices and chillies.

- Cooking with fish (e.g. learning how to skin and fillet fish), meat, game, shellfish, vegetables.

- Pasta day (learning how to make pasta and sauces).

- Men in the kitchen day.

- Cooking for children and with children from scratch.

- Entertaining at home day.

- Vegetarian day.

- Tapas day.

- Simple starters.

- Party desserts.

- Party buffets.

- Party canapés.

- How to get through Christmas as the family cook.

- Demo masterclass by the restaurant's chef(s).

- Ask a local celebrity chef/food writer to do a demonstration.

The most popular cookery courses are Christmas, men, children and entertaining, but other subjects can easily grab the imagination if presented well and clearly on paper. Calculate your costs carefully before deciding on a price per person. Offer discounts for group bookings: one comes free if he or she books six friends, for example. Make sure your classes measure up to expectations, i.e. don't promise more than you can fulfil. Ask your students to fill in a questionnaire before departure for feedback. You may be surprised how much good market research you can achieve.

Outside catering

Your kitchen is an obvious place to capitalise on your assets as well as your skills and those of your staff. Outside catering as well as cookery classes are ways forward during quiet times. Or you may be able to offer your restaurant customers and others who you target a full year-round outside catering service if you have enough space, equipment and staff.

◆ Do work out carefully what the staff and space can handle.

◆ Plan your outside catering menus around these constraints.

◆ You might be able to offer: hot and cold food; a canapé and buffet service; three-course sit-down meals; full wedding parties; a hamper service for sporting or musical events; extra chefs and waiting staff.

◆ Consider whether you will hire or buy in equipment, if you have separate space for storage of food and drink for outside catering, and think about refrigeration and hygiene matters.

◆ Will you be able to give a fair share of your time to discuss outside catering clients' needs? It can be time-consuming, with visits to the client's house or where the party is to be held to be included in your schedule.

◆ Make a supply list, a work schedule, plan transportation and staffing.

◆ Communication with the client is everything. Failure to do this may jeopardise the party and your reputation.

◆ The day after the party can also mean clearing up and sorting out equipment.

- Don't jeopardise your restaurant by taking on too much too soon.

- If you decide to do outside catering or takeaway service, have printed catering menus for customers to pick up.

- Open accounts with companies for breakfasts, lunches, special events or takeaway trade. Make provisos such as payment terms of 30 days, trade references, and stipulate a minimum order and a 24-hour cancellation notice.

But first the essentials

Marketing, selling, planning and organisation are essential tools.

1. Do your homework first. What do local catering companies offer?

2. Identify your market and communicate with them by letter, flyers etc.

3. Create business cards and general menus to go onto flyers.

4. Don't give out prices over the phone but offer the caller a tailor-made menu to be sent in writing after initial discussion of the event, with several price and menu alternatives.

5. Have all the arrangements in writing and agreed on both sides.

6. Ask for a deposit. Some outside caterers ask for 1/3rd when booking, 1/3rd two weeks in advance and the balance on the day of the event. Others ask for ten per cent when the booking takes place, then half minus the ten per cent, then the balance on the day. If dealing with corporate clients you may decide on invoicing them after the event, following an initial deposit.

7. Inform your client of a deposit forfeit should the party be cancelled.

8. Inform your client too of cancellation charges closer to the event.

9. Also inform them of the need to know final numbers one week before the party.

10. Keep any letters of recommendation and testimonials to show to prospective clients.

11. Take photographs of food, events and staff for your records and for marketing.

12. Keep the dialogue going by contacting customers who you have sent information to. Don't expect to win them all though!

Corporate lunches

Service, service, service can often supersede location, location, location thanks to a fast turnaround at lunchtime in the restaurant trade. Business lunches need to be snappy and well managed. It is, therefore, worth considering attracting this market if your restaurant is close to a number of large or medium-sized businesses.

Draw up a list of businesses in the area. Contact the administration or human resources department and find out a name to write to. Prepare a welcoming letter outlining what you can offer the company at lunchtime or for other corporate entertaining, either at your restaurant or as outside catering at the business.

Discuss with your chef (or you may be the chef) the type of dishes that can be offered with swiftness and good value in mind. Prepare some sample menus and send them with the welcoming letter to the member of staff you have located, adding business cards and copies of good reviews or testimonials from other companies. Cold starters and desserts are obvious choices that can be quickly plated. Simply cooked main courses such as grilled fish, meat and pasta are ideal. A simple plate of the best charcuterie with pickles and salads is also popular.

◆ **TOP TIP** ◆

A glass of wine or soft drink and coffee are added incentives within the price per person, but beware. If you offer them poor quality wine or coffee to keep costs down repeat business may not happen.

Some restaurants, like Bistro Montparnasse in Portsmouth, offer a lunch which offers little in the way of profit to them. The reason? This lunch is to showcase what the restaurant can offer. Business people will return in the evening with friends and family for a more relaxed meal, having been assured of good food and service. This is excellent marketing.

You may be able to offer food delivery to companies' boardrooms. Offer food like croissants filled with ham and cheese, cream cheese and crispy bacon, tortilla wraps with a mix of fish, meat and vegetarian fillings, salad bowls, specialist bread sandwiches, bite-size fruit bowls and drinks.

Set up corporate credit accounts, stipulate a minimum order with 24-hours notice and a 24-hour cancellation notice to safeguard your business and your blood pressure!

Writing a column or a cookbook

These are two excellent means of keeping your restaurant's profile in the media market place. But you must examine your skills and your time. Can you write clearly, concisely and interestingly? Will your column's recipes be user-friendly for the general public? Think whether you can fit in the writing as well as cooking and/or running a restaurant, and whether you have something offbeat or unusual to impart in a cookbook.

If you believe that you have many of these attributes here are some steps to take:

◆ Contact your local paper, magazine or radio station and talk to the features editor or programme producer about a column.

◆ Or find out their name and write to them outlining what you have in mind.

◆ Write a one-page letter, outlining your column in clear, concise language and your culinary attributes and other background which may be of interest – but only if relevant. No need to add your five A levels, your prowess at mountain walking, your bookbinding course.

◆ Go to a good bookstore and look at the cookbooks on offer.

◆ Which books would you like to emulate and why? Get their publishers' names.

♦ Highlight a good story you have to tell about your restaurant: how you grow your own vegetables, herbs and salads, raise chickens for the pot, all in the back of beyond. Describe your expertise with unusual puddings or terrines, your exotic culinary pzazz, or that yours has been a family-run restaurant for generations, for example.

♦ Contact the commissioning editors by name either in writing or by phone.

♦ Invest in *The Writer's Handbook* (MacMillan www.panmacmillan.com) for UK publishers, agents, national and regional newspapers and other useful information or *The Guardian Media Guide* (Atlantic Books) for similar guidance and other media information. Both available at large bookstores.

♦ Contact the Guild of Food Writers (www.gfw.co.uk) for advice.

♦ It takes time and perseverance to get on this particular ladder, as I can testify to, but dogged determination can pay off (as I can testify to!).

Don'ts:

♦ Do not write complex recipes to which only chefs can aspire.

♦ Do not write a book unless you have a distinctive, different 'voice'.

♦ Do not take on too much media work – writing a column, a book, tv, radio – as it may take you away from those stoves for too long, and your business will suffer as a result.

8

Staffing for the Well-Run Restaurant

Good restaurants create good, consistent, well-sourced food in a pleasing atmosphere with service to match. In order to achieve this, chefs and front of house staff must be equally creative, consistent, welcoming and professional. And calm.

Temperamental chefs of course exist – and not only on television – but these people are best avoided as no one around them can operate in such an atmosphere and do their best cooking or other kitchen work. Their attitude rubs off on other staff in the restaurant too so choose your chefs – and other staff – prudently. Front of house managers can be equally controlling.

Intimidating verbal behaviour and especially physical abuse are not to be tolerated in the kitchen or restaurant. These traits rightly belong to the past.

Staff, as most restaurateurs will testify, are the biggest problem *and* the biggest asset a restaurant can have.

562,700 jobs were taken by catering staff in 2004, employment in Britain topping 25 million. Nearly 142,000 jobs were filled by men, over 93,000 by women. This was reversed by part-timers (117,700 by men, 209,800 by women).

This chapter deals with:

◆ a broad outlook on staffing problems;

◆ college and agency recruitment;

◆ catering management;

◆ interviewing and job descriptions;

◆ an explanation of kitchen hierarchy;

◆ job commitment;

◆ staff organisation and training;

◆ pay legalities;

◆ job analysis and empowering staff;

◆ basic waiting and management skills, table reservations by staff and duty and cleaning rotas.

It also covers dress code, staff meals, holidays, smoking, behaviour and how to communicate effectively with customers. But first an overview.

THE IMPORTANCE OF SERVICE

Service, service, service is fast overtaking location, location, location in today's competitive restaurant marketplace. As standards rise in quality produce and comfort, so must the service which, of course, covers all kitchen, waiting and cleaning staff and any other employees in a restaurant business.

Personal service and attention to detail set the best restaurants apart from the rest. This applies to the smallest café, the out of the way gastro pub, a town centre or neighbourhood restaurant or wine bar.

We have entered a period of high demand of good staffing due to the booming restaurant trade, but this labour supply needs to come from somewhere. Will potential employees be trained sufficiently to offer good service and high standards? This is of concern for all restaurateurs, even those at the top of the business.

The right mix

What is the ideal mix in a restaurant situation? There is no doubt that the work is demanding, seen negatively by some as relentless, while others see it as a challenge which is both stimulating and rewarding.

Restaurants are sometimes seen as theatre: restaurant staff forming a bond with staff and customers (cast members), the restaurant itself the stage and the work as lines to be learnt. Many exponents of this profession love to entertain, but they must always remember their serious professional stance coupled with humour, good judgement and sensitivity.

Staff need direction, motivation and incentive to carry out their work and to understand the need to be very flexible. This comes from management.

Front of house staff

Front of house staff need to be accepted by both sexes, have the ability to make customers feel at ease and to be trusted for their judgement.

Waiting staff

Waiters – skilled ones – offer service, they know their menu and are aware of the power to make a meal one to remember – or to forget. They are not servants. They have talked to the kitchen about the composition of the food and are able to advise which combinations go best together if the customer isn't sure what to choose. Two cream dishes in succession are to be avoided, for example.

They are aware when to clear a table and when not to. When to pour wine. When a customer is getting restless for the bill. They are also aware of tips and how to generate this extra income. Anyone can wait on tables, but just how natural are they and are they an asset to your business or demolishing it?

Kitchen staff

Kitchen staff are creative in different ways. Chefs have the ability to prepare food, timing cooking to a split second with speed and accuracy. They can cook and present all dishes coming out of the kitchen with skill. And they must be able to do it time and time again to the same high standard. Consistency is all.

FINDING STAFF

Catering colleges are one source of kitchen staffing, but the standard in some is decidedly questionable. The teaching focuses on hotel-like service which is past its sell-by date according to employers.

Flour-based sauces, soups and stocks made from packets and heavy, stodgy food are so out of kilter with today's food styles. This is compounded by outmoded silver service (useful perhaps for banqueting) and folding napkins into unnecessary shapes, amongst other contentious catering issues.

Some colleges have moved on thankfully, and are teaching their students the art of lighter cooking combined with slow-food cooking (daubes, terrines, bread-making for example). They are sourcing their materials with care and attention, and teaching how to run a kitchen, amongst other modern and commercial necessities.

These are the chefs who will be able to deliver the consistently high standards that customers expect and good restaurateurs wish to achieve.

However, some students, when leaving college, feel they wasted their time. The real world can present quite a different aspect of their chosen profession and they have to start the learning process all over again.

Restaurant employers are also handicapped by some students' and non-trained staff's backgrounds. The type of food they experience at home can be quite at variance with food offered in restaurants which they may have no interest in. There can be a mountain to climb in food education, but when a staff member sees the light and becomes excited about the type and quality of the food and service it's a eureka moment.

This is a bleak outlook, I am aware. Staffing is a growing problem due to the fast food nation of eaters who know or care little about cooking, or who come from a background of not eating as a family around a table. Some entering the profession see the catering trade as a way to becoming famous – and fast – to follow in the shoes of the Jamie Olivers of this world without having to work too hard. Unlike Jamie, who started from the bottom of the heap and proved himself.

If at interview stage prospective staff ask how much they will get paid and how much time off they will get, without asking pertinent questions about the restaurant and the job then it's hardly worth continuing the dialogue.

Sources of recruitment

So how to overcome this problem of kitchen staffing? A small restaurant needs a good chef who is able to communicate and teach his or her perhaps younger staff. They need to be able to instil a passion about sourcing excellent produce, and cooking it with skill and care. Apprenticeship is alive and well and should be encouraged vigorously with many students attending day release courses while working in a restaurant kitchen.

◆ TOP TIP ◆

Train local people to deliver the goods. Create a good team by encouraging their creative side but with good, solid guidelines laid down either by management or by a head chef. Kitchens that work well are staffed by local people who enjoy being together and creating good food and service.

Be they local or recruited from further afield, they must be able to cover for one another in time of crisis or staff absence, making sure that the whole service runs as smoothly and as pleasantly as possible. Never hire whingers, clock watchers or lazy people. These traits could be difficult to assess at interview, granted. They can infect a good team.

Recruitment agencies

Catering agencies are employment agencies but dedicated to this specific industry. They may place permanently or temporarily. There may be 30,000 vacancies on any one day in London alone due to the burgeoning restaurant and hotel market. Job vacancies include head chefs, trainees, commis and sous chefs, kitchen porters, waiters and waitresses, bar staff and managers.

An agency charges at least ten per cent of the agreed wage, the chef or other member of staff via the agency working a probationary period. On completion, the agency will invoice the company for their percentage.

It is important to weigh up the costs and advantages if you are recruiting agency staff. On the plus side, many agencies get to know their applicants well and match appropriate chefs to appropriate businesses. It's not in their interests to get this wrong but, of course, it can and does happen, as some agencies see the chef as merely making money for them. Agencies aren't cheap and you may achieve just as good if not better results with an ad which may attract greater numbers of applicants.

Temporary agency staff usually are better paid per hour. This may cause friction once it is known by your other staff if their hourly rate doesn't match the temp's pay, so try not to enter this mix if humanly possible.

Promote from within. It is easier and more cost effective to find a commis chef from an agency than going to an agency to recruit a higher up position. The chef may be able to train up a commis chef who has been with the company for a while to the higher grade.

Other sources

◆ advertising;

◆ job centres;

- headhunters;

- existing staff;

- waiting list – people coming to the restaurant looking for a job;

- previous applicants;

- casual callers;

- education systems.

MOTIVATION

Is catering management unique? Every industry thinks it is unique and in a sense, each is right. A look at the industry, with its uniforms, differing job titles, tipping, unsocial hours, labour mobility, irregular work flow, and the degree of entrepreneurship needed in the restaurant business demonstrates that the catering industry is certainly a special case.

Due to this 'special case' scenario, one thing is for sure: you must be organised. And that means good staffing at all levels, staff who are flexible, understand speed when busy but do not forego quality. They must have the ability to do other jobs such as cleaning and undergo extra training if necessary during less busy times. Motivation by management is paramount to keeping good staff. Job satisfaction cannot be underestimated.

Unskilled staff

What motivates those without skills? The reasons why unskilled catering work is popular are:

- The work is easy to learn.

- There is variety.

- It is not a factory.

- You meet people.

- It is convenient to get quick money and doesn't have to be permanent.

How to motivate people

It is necessary to introduce good housekeeping practices with staff in order to keep them. It is done by:

- Clear communication. It is not possible to respond positively when clarity isn't present.

- Not over-controlling.

- Recognising achievement. This will result in increased good performance.

- Good teaching.

- Rewarding adequately.

- Reviewing performance on a regular basis.

- Treating staff like human beings and not like cogs in a machine.

- Avoiding promises and favours and then not delivering them.

- Taking what people say seriously. Listening to staff.

- Investigating complaints or grievances.

- Avoiding deals.

- Making your staff realise you are a real team.

- Recognising a career commitment.

The attachment to working as a team may be because:

- They have something in common rather than working for the same business, eg they are all students, all women, all the same age.

- Working on these shared characteristics and building up their bond.

Commitment to the job can also be achieved by staff being prepared to ditch old skills and learn new ones, thereby empowering them and recognising their assets. Loyalty and flexibility may be the outcome.

THE STAFF INTERVIEW

The relationship between employer and employee may start when the manager says 'start Monday' and the applicant says 'OK'. But what agreement has been come to?

Getting off to a good start

At the interview stage, the interviewer is keen to assess the capabilities of the interviewee re effort, general willingness and track record (if not taking on a novice in the business). At that 'start Monday' stage, the agreement is very imprecise and open to misinterpretation.

The employer is taking on an unspecified potential, the employee an indeterminate amount of work. Good interviewing practice, job descriptions, previous experience of the same type of work and the taking up of references all create a more precise and mutual understanding.

However, a job description can't describe what effort will be required and is therefore imprecise. But all the usual conditions such as the work entailed, hours of work, shift times, payment, staff meals, behaviour and dress can be defined and clarified in a job description.

Therefore, it is a good idea to take on a willing applicant for a **trial period** before offering a permanent job.

If taking on new chefs, ask them to cook a dish or two from your menu then sit down with them and, over the tasting, discuss with them the outcome and what they would be able to contribute to the menu and style of cooking.

Although this may seem like a lengthy process, at least you will be able to choose a good chef rather than one who may look good on paper but can't cook the simplest of dishes. And it will save you time and money in the long run.

During this process, you will be able to find out if the chef is familiar with and knows how to cook the ingredients on your menu. If the chef is unable to rise to the challenge of cooking steamed sea bass with a fennel sauce, for example, or even the best omelette, then you may not be talking the same culinary language.

To circumvent this procedure and to save time and money, find out as much as possible over the phone or by other means of communication before agreeing to an interview – and the cook-off.

Culinary checklist

You may also wish to have a culinary checklist asking, for example: What is your strongest area? Is there any section of the kitchen you feel less secure in?

Some possible subjects for the checklist:

Which can you cook?/cooked in your last job?

◆ patés and terrines;

◆ soups;

◆ breads;

◆ canapés;

◆ ice creams;

◆ sauces;

◆ dressings;

◆ game;

◆ fish;

◆ egg dishes: omelettes, eg Eggs Benedict;

◆ butchery;

◆ larder experience;

- working out GP – the kitchen's gross profits;

- menu costing;

- purchasing.

Don't underestimate the applicant who applies for a job without qualifications and experience. If the person displays a real enthusiasm and knowledge of food, and has a passion for cooking and learning, they may be just the one to take on for a trial period. He or she may just have that creative side that those with certificates lack.

The objectives of the employment interview

- To decide if the applicant is suitable for the job or, conversely, how suitable the job is for the applicant.

- To decide if the applicant will fit into the existing team and into the organisation.

- To get across the essential expectations and requirements of the job. The interview can be seen as part of the induction process.

- To gather information, evaluate it and make a judgement.

- To find out the applicant's skills, experience and character.

- To assess the interest of the applicant in the business.

Ask open questions, not ones that can only yield a yes or a no:

- Tell me about your present job.

- What do you enjoy most about your job?

- Can you give me some examples?

- What did you enjoy about college?

- What did you get out of it?

- What made you decide to apply for the job?

- How do you find dealing with staff?

- Have you ever dealt with an uncooperative employee and what was the outcome?

- How do you feel about moving to this part of the country?

- How will this affect your home life?

When interviewing staff for either kitchen or front of house ask for references and *follow them up*.

During the interview

Do get across to potential staff the kind of high standards you expect from them including dress, cleanliness (are those nails and shoes clean?), behaviour (fag breaks are few and far between, for example, and not within eyesight of customers, either inside or out). Their flexibility (can they be called upon to do shifts at short notice?), their attitude to customers and the necessity of teamwork.

Find out if they are familiar with the type of food on offer and are willing to learn. Do they understand about wine and drinks service? If not, are they keen to find out? Can they work under pressure? With a smile? Are they motivated? Do they like working as part of a team? Do they look at you in the eye?

Or you may sense that they are only working for the money and will be out the door when the shift ends, not willing to add to the harmony and efficiency of the restaurant if extra tidying up, paperwork for example, is necessary.

Do you in turn give the impression of good management and organisation? Do you offer a decent wage according to experience and skills? Do you come across as a caring person who staff can come to in times of need? Are you approachable? Do you give enough information about your staff needs and expectations? Or will you spring something on them that wasn't mentioned in interview after they have started working for you? You should offer a clear, concise contract with hours, duties and pay structure.

If an employee is to respond to customers' needs they must know what the product or service is, its full breadth and its limits; what the business can do and cannot do as false promises to customers – and staff – can end in tears and recrimination.

They also need to know the rules of the organisation, and how to be sensitive and discreet.

This knowledge must be given to the employee and not found out by chance. Careful role definition and training is a necessity.

OTHER EMPLOYMENT TIPS

Draw up a job description

No matter how simple or low-level the job, the more information you put down, the better your chances of getting the right person for the job. Cover areas such as skills needed, any necessary training, and how much experience and responsibility the job requires.

References

Always take up references before someone joins your business. For a fuller, more in depth reply, phone the referee and ask questions such as 'would you re-employ this person?'.

Make your employees feel welcome

First impressions count and the first three months of employment with a new boss, new colleagues and work are very important. Make your new employee feel welcome. Don't just pass them by and say 'are you all right?' Spend a few minutes with them to find out if they are feeling included, the job not giving them difficulties but pleasure and satisfaction – or the reverse. Give praise where it is due. Keep a list of their birthdays and either wish them 'happy birthday' or give them a card (if the business isn't too huge to handle this act of kindness).

◆ TOP TIP ◆

A business is only as good as the people who work for it.

If you run a small business you will be closer to your staff, suppliers and customers than in larger ones. Involve your employees in the work culture from day one and keep them up to date with the progress of the restaurant, especially any plans for future developments. Finding out from a third party can lead to disenchantment.

Appraise your staff regularly

Include a review system for each staff member. The business may have changed, perhaps creating more work for your staff. They may be finding it difficult to absorb without a dip in quality and service. Discuss any issues with the full team present.

Enforce strict 'absence' procedures

In order to deal effectively with absenteeism and late arrival at work, staff should be very clear about company policy. A staff handbook is an ideal way to state policies clearly, even if it is done on an in-house computer rather than going to the expense of printing it.

Areas such as holidays, sickness, absenteeism, lateness, dress code, make-up, jewellery, hair colour, type of shoes, smoking policy and using mobile phones at work should be included and clearly outlined. This applies to restaurants of all sizes.

Overtime

A couple of phone calls and you have arranged for some overtime with existing staff. Simple. But overtime can run out of control. First, it can undermine quality of service and secondly, it can undermine recruitment.

For example, people like to earn more but tiredness can and does set in. Patterns of good work turn into just getting by, with staff going through the motions and taking short cuts.

The longer the vacancy exists for that extra staff member, the more existing staff get used to the extra money. When recruitment does take place and a new member joins the team, he or she may be resented as wages decrease for those on overtime.

Be aware and take action if a new member of staff is required to be taken on so that overtime doesn't spiral out of control. Its by-products will be a lowering of standards and creeping inefficiency.

EMPLOYING PEOPLE

When employing people the first thing to do is to call the New Employers' Helpline on (0845) 60 70 143. The adviser will set up an employment record and send an Employer's Starter Pack with all the information you need. Or you can arrange help on payroll from a business adviser from a local Business Support Team.

All services are free and you can also attend one of the local workshops on payroll. Phone them or contact via www.inlandrevenue.gov.uk/bst/index.htm

As an employer you will be responsible for:

◆ Working out the tax and National Insurance contributions due each pay day.

◆ Keeping accurate and up to date records to back up any deduction in your accounts for wages, payments, benefits and such-like relating to your employees.

◆ Making payments of Statutory Sick and Maternity pay to your employees as appropriate.

◆ Making Student Loan deductions from an employee's earnings when directed by the Inland Revenue.

◆ Paying Tax Credits to employees when directed by the Inland Revenue.

◆ Paying deductions made over to the Inland Revenue Accounts Office each month – or quarterly if your average monthly payments are below £1,500 – after offsetting any tax credit payments.

◆ At the end of the tax year (April 5) telling the Inland Revenue how much each of your employees has earned, and how much tax and NIC (National Insurance Contributions) deductions you have made. You must also give details of any expenses paid or benefits provided to your employees.

Useful telephone numbers and websites:

Help with PAYE (Pay As You Earn) and/or NIC (National Insurance Contributions) for New Employers (0845) 60 70 143.

National Minimum Wage Helpline (0845) 600 0678.

Employers' orderline for forms and stationery orders (08457) 646 646.

Useful leaflets and pamphlets via www.inlandrevenue.gov.uk

The law on pay and hours of work

Legislation is based on British labour law and European social policy for working hours and minimum pay levels, the focus being on:

◆ limiting working hours;

◆ protection from pressure to work excessive hours;

◆ guaranteed holiday pay;

◆ guaranteed rest periods;

◆ guaranteed minimum pay.

National Minimum Wage

An employer must pay a general minimum rate of at least £4.85 an hour for workers over 22 years old.

For workers aged 18–21 and for workers aged 22 or over for six months after starting a new job with a new employer and receiving accredited training, the minimum rate is £4.10 an hour.

Youth workers: 16–17 years of age: £3 an hour.

These rates came into force on October 1 2004.

For more information contact www.tiger.gov.uk

Working time and pay regulations

An employer must not require workers or employees to work more than an average of 48 hours a week, though workers and employees may choose to work longer.

◆ An employer must limit the normal working hours of night workers to an average of eight hours in any 24-hour period. Although this doesn't affect restaurants as such presently, there may be restaurants in the future that open 24 hours.

◆ An entitlement to daily, weekly and in-work rest and four weeks' paid annual leave.

◆ Under the Employment Rights Act 1996 an employer must provide all employees with an individual written pay statement at or before the time of payment. It must show gross pay and take-home pay with amounts and reasons for variable and fixed deductions. Or, fixed deductions can be shown as a total sum, provided a written statement of these items is given in advance to each employee at least once a year.

◆ An employer must not make unauthorised deductions from wages including complete non-payment.

Part-time workers' regulations

This is very applicable to the restaurant business where many staff members are part-timers. The regulations are poorly adhered to unfortunately, but the following must be observed.

Part-time employees are not to be treated less favourably than full-time employees, their contractual terms and conditions equal in pay, pensions, annual holidays and training.

Further information: www.dti.gov.uk/er/ptime.htm

Employing foreign nationals

The nationals of the following new member states of the European Economic Area (EEA) have been free to come to the UK to work from 1 May 2004: Poland, Lithuania, Estonia, Latvia, Slovenia, Slovakia, Hungary and the Czech Republic. Nationals who find a job are required to register with the Home Office under the new Worker Registration Scheme as soon as they find work.

If they plan to work for more than one month for a UK employer they need to register. Once they have been working legally in the UK for 12 months without a break, they will have full rights of free movement.

Those from Austria, Belgium, Cyprus, Italy, Liechtenstein, Denmark, Finland, France, Germany, Greece, Iceland, Ireland, Malta, Netherlands, Norway, Spain and Sweden have been able to work freely in the UK since membership of the EEA.

Nationals from Cyprus and Malta have full free movement rights and are not required to obtain a workers registration certificate.

Many Australians, New Zealanders, Canadians and other Commonwealth nationals come to Britain to work, with a good number of them working in the restaurant trade. Under the Working Holidaymakers Scheme 17–30 year olds may work in Britain for two years. They may work full or part-time and can apply once only and must have the stamp or endorsement clearly marked on their passport for the employer to check.

For a full list of Commonwealth members and for other information regarding employing foreign nationals, obtain *Comprehensive Guidance for United Kingdom Employers on Changes in the Law on Preventing Illegal Working* from www.ind.homeoffice.gov.uk. It can be downloaded. Or call the Employers' Helpline (0845) 010 6677 for a booklet.

If you have employed a foreign national, the way to obtain a National Insurance number is for them to attend an 'evidence of identity' interview at the nearest job centre, taking with them their passport or proof of identity as well as evidence that they are working. For further details contact www.workingintheuk.gov.uk

Maternity rights

Many stories are carried by the media on the flouting of the laws concerning pregnant employees, so avoid causing a legal hassle by following these points:

◆ Employers are required to protect the health and safety of employees who are pregnant, have recently given birth or are breast-feeding.

◆ These protections start as soon as the employee is pregnant.

◆ The contract of employment throughout the 18 weeks' ordinary maternity leave or any additional leave must be continued unless either party to the contract ends it or it expires.

◆ During maternity leave the employee should continue to receive all her contractual benefits except wages.

◆ An employer must not dismiss an employee or select her for redundancy in preference to other comparable employees during her pregnancy or maternity leave just because she is pregnant.

◆ For further information: www.dti.gov.uk/er/maternity.htm

Redundancy payment

An employer who dismisses an employee by reason of redundancy is required to make a lump sum payment to the employee based on his or her age, length of service and rate of pay at the time of dismissal.

For further information contact (0870) 1502 500 or the Department of Trade and Industry's website: www.dti.gov.uk/regs

Unfair dismissal

Employees who believe they have been unfairly dismissed can complain to an employment tribunal, generally subject to a qualifying period of one year's continuous service. Complaints can be made regardless of length of service if the dismissal is for certain specified reasons, eg pregnancy or maternity leave.

Trade union membership

All employees have a right to belong, or not belong, to a trade union. It is unlawful to refuse a person employment because he or she either is or is not a member of a trade union. It is also unlawful for employees to be dismissed or discriminated against because of their membership or non-membership of a trade union.

Staff meals

One of the worst signals you can give your staff is to palm them off with a poor meal while on duty. What it says to them is that you don't place a value on them. And how else will they learn about the food they are preparing and serving if they aren't offered it? They will have much more respect for you if given a meal that is nourishing, delicious and shared by all at table before service.

Jill Dupleix, the *Times* newspaper cook and author, passed by London's Kensington Place restaurant and spied staff sitting down to huge bowls of penne with meatballs and a green salad and is all for this good practice.

Another meal at Zilli Fish in Covent Garden was equally admired by Jill as staff ate a roasting tray of fat sardines sizzling in garlic and tomatoes, spaghetti with a chilli sauce, and roasted red peppers and chicken thighs with a pizzaiola-style sauce.

In other words, it doesn't have to cost the earth. Quite the reverse, as demonstrated by these simple dishes. A good meal helps to create a happier team. And if waiting staff eat some of the dishes on the menu they will be better prepared to sell it having also understood the process undergone by the cooking.

I passionately agree that restaurateurs should feed their staff well. It was one reason for my staff feeling included and well looked after, not just another cog in the wheel. I loved their awakening to different foods and styles of cooking. They were able to describe the food in more detail to customers who in turn felt confident about the ethos of the restaurant. However altruistic this may seem it also helped them to broaden their outlook and to feel part of a strong team.

KITCHEN HIERARCHY TERMINOLOGY EXPLAINED

The professional kitchen's cooking staff are known as the **brigade**. Like many kitchen words, it comes from the French and, further back, *brigata*, from the Italian, a company or crew, so its origins are military.

Look up the word in an Italian dictionary and ironically you'll find it from the verb *brigare*, 'to brawl, wrangle or fight'.

The ideal restaurant staff

The size of the brigade is dependent on the establishment. Many small restaurants are based on a head chef, a sous chef and/or a commis chef plus, hopefully, a kitchen porter whose job is mainly to wash up.

Or staff may be simply the chef, relying on perhaps waiting staff to help out with washing up and lesser preparations like plating desserts, prepping breads, butter and ancilliaries.

Large restaurants will have an executive chef, head chef, senior and junior sous (under, literally: French), chefs, chefs de partie (those responsible for a section of the kitchen, (eg sauces, larder, starters, mains, vegetables and desserts), demi-chefs de partie (literally half), commis (first and second) chef. A commis, a deputy or clerk, learns his or her trade from the bottom of the hierarchy. They are there to help, learn and watch.

There may also be a (rare) chef tournant, an all-purpose chef who is capable of all sections and who may be filling in for absent/holidaying chefs.

Definitions from the lowest rank to the highest rank:

Kitchen porter

Have respect for the KP, as they are affectionately known. Their job is an unenviable one of washing pots, utensils, glasses, plates – the lot – and they may also be offered the joys of prepping vegetables and washing salads. Be kind to the kitchen porter as he or she must endure repetitive tasks, which are the underpinning of the system.

The commis chef

OK, not the dream job envisaged by some but this is the job to learn by. Duties may include plating up garnishes for all courses, with some cooking involved including stocks. Depending on the size of the restaurant they may deal with stock-taking and deliveries.

Demi chef de partie

This is the next step up: running a station with more responsibilities. It is the time for the chef to prove him or herself and show a willingness to learn and work.

Chef de partie

Literally 'head of a team', the next quasi-military full rank up with the ability to organise other chefs. This is a managerial step up. In a small restaurant a chef de partie may be in charge of just one chef or several in a large one. Duties could include staff meals, sauces, meat and fish prep, hot starters.

Sous chef

This is the head chef's immediate number two and capable of doing the head chef's job in his or her absence. In a larger kitchen there may be a junior or senior sous chef, in a smaller one just the sous (under or sub) chef.

In a big kitchen, the sous chef virtually manages and does little cooking due to managing the kitchen, people, office work, rotas, food ordering, training: it is a position of authority. A junior sous chef is part chef, part manager.

Head chef

The head chef in any sized kitchen is in charge. His or her only superior is the executive head chef who may be in charge of several restaurants, either independent ones or within a large company or establishment such as a hotel.

In a small restaurant, the chef is responsible for all cooking, ordering, management and training.

The head chef's jobs are to create menus, write the recipes or guidelines to go with the recipes, find the best suppliers, recruit, discipline and promote staff. In the absence of a sous chef, he or she is also responsible for rotas, giving out specific jobs such as larder work, cleaning, cooking, management, and making sure the kitchen is up to scratch re hygiene and health inspections.

He or she is also responsible for reporting to overall management, discussing future strategies, any special holiday catering such as Christmas or weddings, banqueting, dealing with customer and staff issues and stock-taking checks. Liaison with front of house staff may be delegated to the sous chef.

THE KITCHEN CAREER

Depending on the type of job offered and sought after, working in a restaurant kitchen can take many directions. For a commis chef who latches onto a goal and works through a tough time, it can seem insuperable but worth it under a good head chef for this period of learning.

A commis working outside a large conurbation is part of a small brigade and works in all stations. He or she may learn more quickly – and well – if the head chef is good and eager to pass on knowledge and expertise.

In large cities and in a large restaurant/hotel a commis chef might find the whole process more daunting due to the sheer numbers in the kitchen, and will stay only if given the right treatment in the establishment. But they can move on to other restaurants crying out for staff at this level – and will if the money and treatment are better.

The fast track to learning in the business is to be a commis in a good, small restaurant with maybe four or five chefs and being introduced to all stages of cooking. Finding commis chefs who are willing to learn and committed to the job is of paramount importance, in particular to the small or medium-sized restaurant.

Financially, it is not viable to have several chefs of the same ranking unless business is booming, hence the importance of a keen (and less well paid) commis chef. But do see beyond the cooking skills when interviewing for this position as described in Interviewing Staff. The right attitude is of equal importance.

Women chefs

Who says they can't take the pace? There is this myth around – circulated by misogynists – that women aren't strong enough, can't stand the bad language and have an unfortunate attitude to getting on in the kitchen. They cry a lot, they can't lift heavy stock pots, they are moody because of their periods. They can't stand the pace and get flustered easily. Poppycock!

Women have a lot to prove – still – in this male-dominated trade. Many are perceived as being only good as pastry chefs. The discrimination is still quite breath-taking. This is perhaps why I opened and ran a restaurant for eight years in Sussex as chef/owner rather than work for unsympathetic, bullying characters. Of course it is a demanding job but we women can hack it, and offer many good traits to men, attention to detail being just one.

Witness head chefs Sally Clarke (Clarke's), Angela Hartnett (The Connaught), Ruth Rogers and Rose Gray (River Café), Samantha Clark, (Moro), Helena Poulakka (Sonny's), all in London, Sonia Brooke-Little, Churchill Arms, Paxford, Gloucestershire, and Shirley Spear and Isobel Tomlin at the Three Chimneys, Isle of Skye. They represent some of the many excellent women head chefs in Britain.

KITCHEN AND FRONT OF HOUSE STAFF WORKING TOGETHER

Management is responsible for getting the relationship balance right or, at least, recognising the differing tensions within these two groups and settling any disputes and grievances that can build up.

The old adage that the customer is always right can be challenged here when it comes to food. When it is ready, it is at its peak condition and should be served immediately, not when the customer wishes to vacate the bar at his or her own time. This is where skilled waiting comes in. The waiter is the one who seats the customer and is aware of the order of priority the kitchen is working in.

+ The waiter judges the timing of each table and reports back to the kitchen if diners are taking an inordinate amount of time over the first course, for example. Or, conversely, if faster service is required and is possible to achieve.

+ A mutual respect must be built up between kitchen and front of house staff. If the latter doesn't understand the former's work pattern and degree of skill in putting each dish together then trust, confidence and ability to communicate effectively break down.

+ This is where management comes in and, indeed, where it should have come in beforehand if sensitive to the atmosphere developing between kitchen and restaurant. Turn the tables and get them to perform each other's work, or at least shadow different sections to understand their challenges and difficulties.

DRESS CODE, SMOKING, BEHAVIOUR AND COMMUNICATING WITH CUSTOMERS

Your front of house staff reflect the kind of restaurant you are running therefore make sure of the following.

Appearance
If staff have a uniform make sure it is clean, pressed, uniform in style and well-fitting. If you operate a no-uniform policy, then stipulate what your

staff should wear and be vigilant as to the characteristics above. Do stipulate too the type of shoes, that they should be in good repair and cleaned regularly, and policy on the wearing of jewellery, make-up, style of hair.

Hygiene

All staff should have short, clean, unvarnished nails and *must* wash their hands after a fag break, going to the loo, returning to duty after going to the shops, handling stock from a van, etc.

All of the above applies too to kitchen staff. The cleanliness of their aprons, chef's jackets and the wearing of head gear are of paramount importance, not only to the overall standards of hygiene but also if seen by customers who will judge the restaurant accordingly.

Smoking

Smoking is a vexed question in the restaurant business as there is a high ratio of smokers to non-smokers who simply can't live without a fag break, it appears. Be strict about these breaks as it is unfair on the non-smokers who have to pick up the slack.

Make sure that smokers are not seen by customers hovering by an open door or by the bins as this really does give a wrong impression.

All smokers should wash their hands before service. If there is an all-pervading smell of smoking it can be a real turn-off for the customer (smoky clothes, breath, hands). But banning smoking by staff can be tantamount to calling for a mutiny. You may be fortunate enough to employ non-smokers but, if not, be a vigilant manager/owner.

Drugs

If you suspect any staff member has a drug problem, deal with it. If they come in late, don't turn up at all or show signs of drug and alcohol abuse, do you really want this kind of behaviour in your restaurant? No.

Music

Music is often turned up for the benefit of staff who seemingly can't live without it. Staff will also bring in their own type of music to inflict on the suffering public if management again isn't vigilant. Don't let this happen as it can spiral out of control and will soon be seen as a 'right'.

As a restaurant critic I receive many letters from customers, and the subject of music is one of the most contentious issues apart from poor service and terrible food. If customers can't make themselves heard to other diners and staff they will vote with their feet.

Meeting and greeting

Meeting and greeting has to be well pitched. The customer should preferably be met at the door and shown to a table once staff have found out if they have booked or whether they wish to book or make an enquiry.

Do your staff speak English or the language of the restaurant? Can they communicate effectively without that language?

Staff should on no account gather in groups by the bar and ignore that door opening or continue to carry on a personal conversation. As a customer and critic I find this is far too often the case, and the customer is not made to feel welcome or wanted. I often walk out if this happens. There are plenty more restaurants which would welcome the business.

Please say at least hello to the customer. In Britain this seems to be a difficulty. Slamming down the menu in front of the customer and asking in a bored voice – with eyes not even looking in the direction of the customer – what they would like to drink is very off-putting. Instead, look them in the eye, smile, offer a greeting, ask where they would like to sit if this is an option, offer them a menu immediately and find out if they would like a drink or wait until they have chosen from the menu. No hard sell please. Make your customers feel at ease.

Service

A good waiting staff member is able to relate to each table's needs. Business tables, loving couples' tables, a family outing all need different approaches.

Self respect and respect of others is paramount, as are professionalism and efficiency. A good memory is also important.

Make sure waiting staff know what is on the menu and if there are any specials which they can describe, but not in a fast monotone. No one will be taking it in, with the result that the specials won't sell.

Waiting staff must be not only aware of what the dishes consist of but also wines by the glass, their types and what food they go with. They should also be knowledgeable about all the drinks on offer. It should not be just guesswork on their part. What kind of coffee do you buy? What brandies are there?

Waiting staff should make sure that there is sufficient space on the table before serving plates, vegetables, wine bottles, butter, bread and other items. It's no good just pushing things around the table to fit them in, as it creates tension with the customer and a feeling of not being looked after appropriately, a kind of take it or leave it attitude.

When it comes to the bill be aware of people's needs. Watch their body language. Be prepared. Ask if they would like anything more. Be around. Don't buzz off to the kitchen to chat up the sous chef. Keep an unobtrusive eye on those valuable customers.

Lasting impressions: dos and don'ts

Do say goodbye as warmly as you greeted them. This will create a lasting impression. People don't just go to restaurants for a good meal. They go for a good time out, a pleasing atmosphere, good service.

Don't fawn, ingratiate yourself or be over-familiar. Don't be loud or noisy. Don't ever, ever be rude.

- Do be friendly, pleasant, efficient and professional.

- Enjoy yourself, but do keep your fingers off the volume control going clockwise. It's not your party. It's theirs.

◆ TOP TIP ◆

Tips for professional waiting skills

- When seating three people at a table for four, for example, always remove the place setting of cutlery, glasses, side plate, napkin where a fourth person may have sat. This applies to any table size when all seats aren't taken up.

- Hold the plate by placing four fingers under the plate, the thumb on the side and not on the surface of the plate.

- Serve from the left and remove from the right.

- When holding two plates in one hand, balance one plate on the forearm by the wrist, the other underneath with three fingers under the second plate, thumb and small finger on the rim.

- Clear plates by balancing one plate as above for cutlery, the stronger part of the forearm and wrist bearing the weight of the cleared plates.

- Serve drinks on the right where the glass is positioned.

- Serve food without asking 'who's having the paté?' Identify each diner by number, starting perhaps with the one nearest to the bar as number one, then going around clockwise.

- Orders must be written legibly, in capitals preferably, so that kitchen staff can readily identify each dish.

- Always add any other information eg 'medium-rare' clearly, the number of covers, the waiting staff member's name and table number.

- Always hold glasses by their stem, never the bowl unless clearing dirty glasses.

- Clear the table after each course, leaving it set for the next course.

- Always make sure the table is left cleared ready for dessert or coffee with the removal of salt and pepper and unnecessary cutlery, for example.

- Clear plates only when everyone at a table has finished eating. It gives the wrong impression, i.e. you're hurrying them, if cleared at different times, putting the slower eater in a dilemma.

MANAGEMENT SKILLS

A good manager shows self-confidence, has a complete understanding of the operation, maintains a good rapport between kitchen and restaurant and possesses charm. He or she is a leader, takes responsibility and can delegate well but must also be able to be hands-on without undermining other staff, eg showing them up before customers and other staff members.

The same dos and don'ts apply to the manager as well as to waiting staff (see Dress Code, Smoking, Behaviour and Service above).

The manager has ultimate control over the reservations and should plan each session successfully, eg delegating changes of seating to waiting staff to suit a particular party, noting special requirements, informing staff of these requirements.

The manager must be able to create the setting up of a table plan of the restaurant and number each table. It is essential in either a large or small restaurant to achieve the maximum table take-up. This is a skill that comes with practice.

They must be able to create and implement a clear booking plan with space for name, number of covers, time, table number, contact telephone number, and any special requirements or comments about the booking.

They also need to manage a daily seating time plan with times and numbers of guests. They must liase with the chef as to how many customers can be booked in at a specific time, eg 8 pm when the restaurant is at its most hectic. Or how many other tables can be accommodated if large parties are booked in. Balancing time and space is the key.

Make sure that staff write in bookings in a legible way and that all staff know how to take bookings.

STAFF ROTAS

Rotas are a vital tool to any restaurant so that, at a glance, everyone can see who is working or absent. They are made up on a weekly basis but, with good management, they can be worked out four weeks ahead of time, taking into consideration holidays, days off, staff shortages, overtime, busy times of year with more staff required. Include managers in the rota to show that all staff are equal and accountable.

It is important to put your or your chef's managerial skills into practice here and be as fair to all staff members as far as possible. For example, unless specifically asked for, don't pile all the evening work on some staff members. Give them equal numbers of day shifts to their co-workers so they have a night off with their family and friends.

Discuss the rota with all staff and follow up any complaints or dissatisfaction promptly as grievances can build up.

◆ TOP TIP ◆

> Include cleaning and refrigeration temperature checking too on staff rotas so that they are brought to the forefront. They should be seen as a necessary part of the working week, not just something to be fitted in as and when, or done in a desultory fashion or even forgotten.

Print out staff rotas and preferably reprint if there are a number of changes to a rota so that confusion doesn't arise. Otherwise a staff member may not turn up, mistakenly thinking they had swopped duties.

Below is an example of a staff rota for a small restaurant which is closed on Mondays, the sous chef taking over the chef's work on Thursdays, the roles reversed on Tuesdays. There may also be more part-time waiting staff. If the owner is in charge of management he or she will be present most if not all days, but not necessarily all hours. Add these dates and times to the rota.

Staff	Tuesday	Wednesday	Thursday	Friday	Saturday	Sunday
Head Chef	8–2 pm 6–11 pm	10–2 pm 6–11 pm	off	9–2 pm 6–11 pm	10–2 pm 6–11 pm	10–4 pm
Sous chef	Off	10–2 pm 6–11 pm	9–2 pm 6–11 pm	10–2 pm 6–11 pm	10–2 pm 6–11 pm	10–4 pm
KP 1*	9–5	5–11	5–11	9–5	5–11	Off
KP 2*	5–11	Off	9–5	5–11	9–5	9–5 pm
Waiter 1	Off	10–2 pm 6–11 pm	10–2	6–11	10–2 pm 6–11 pm	11–5 pm
Waiter 2	10–2 pm 6–11 pm	off	6–11 pm	10–2 pm 6–11 pm	10–2 pm 6–11 pm	11 – 5 pm

* will also perform cleaning duties in the kitchen, restaurant, toilets.

Cleaning tips

Cleaning is an essential part of any food business. It minimises the risk of food contamination, infestation and provides a pleasant and safe working environment.

To be effective, cleaning must be planned and incorporated into the staff rota:

◆ Adopt a clean-as-you-go policy with spillages and food debris when preparing food.

◆ Draw up a list of all items of equipment and areas for cleaning and how often they need to be cleaned.

◆ A separate list for toilet maintenance and cleaning should also be compiled.

◆ What materials and equipment need to be used for equipment and areas?

◆ Who is responsible for these jobs?

◆ Prepare a comprehensive scheduled programme.

- Review the programme if a new piece of equipment or a new area come into being.

- Store cleaning materials away from all food.

- Keep cleaning materials in their original containers.

- Don't mix cleaning materials as noxious fumes can be given off.

- Never clean an area which is still being used by customers with bleach or other strong-smelling cleaners as the odour is extremely off-putting.

- If strong cleaning smells linger on after opening times find another type of cleaning agent, as customers really do dislike coming into a hospital-type smell and may not stay – or return.

- Wash hands after using any cleaning materials.

9

Designing Menus

The menu – or menus – are the restaurant's raison d'être, the pulling power that brings people in. Watch people surrounding a menu on view outside the door, and they will be weighing up the pros and cons of passing your threshold.

They will have initially peered through the windows to weigh up 'shall we, shan't we enter?' They have taken into account the many attractions laid out before them: the use of space, décor, staff, lighting and the atmosphere already generated by those enjoying the fruits of your labour. And what will determine their final decision? Your menu. On view.

THE IMPORTANCE OF THE MENU

Sometimes taken for granted by restaurateurs, menus showcase the kitchen's abilities and strengths. They represent the coming together of restaurateur, chef, supplier and style of the restaurant.

Once enticed and seated, the customer may ask pertinent questions having had an even more comprehensive look at the menu. Of course repeat business customers know and trust your ethos, but those passers-by need to be wooed, seduced into passing over your threshold. The menu is a hugely important factor not only because of its content but in the way it is set out.

To maximise profit, put your higher-priced items second from the top and second from the bottom as customers tend to order more often from these two locations. Also when reviewing your menu, get rid of dishes that don't sell early on. You don't want any dish not pulling its weight in either revenue, profit or menu balance.

THE MENU: FOOD CONSISTENCY

Now to the food. It has to be consistent. Of course the 'wow' factor is important but even more so is the consistency of the food that emerges from the kitchen to the restaurant. Your customers will desert you in droves if the food on their plate doesn't match the last meals they enjoyed in your business. If the standards are allowed to slip – you get in a chef who likes to create a buzz but can't hack doing a good job day in day out – then you must re-examine your kitchen's strengths.

If you go down the complex food route there is more chance that it will go wrong. If you change your chef, and the replacement is unable to rise to the challenge, then you risk losing your audience if his or her skills are not as great as the previous chef.

Therefore, simplicity is the best way forward, unless you have an exceptionally talented chef who is able to concoct the finest food without a hitch on a daily basis.

But even simplicity demands care and attention to detail. And knowing what goes with what. Just simply throwing a whole lot of good ingredients together without the knowledge of food marriages made in heaven will result in a horrid mishmash of tastes and ill-judged flavours.

The menu war of the sexes

Guy Browning, the *Guardian Weekend*: '… women start at the bottom of a menu and work up. They look for death by chocolate, then justify the end of the meal by seeking out the most lettuce-rich dish at the beginning. Men start in the middle, where they look for the word 'sausage'. Once they've found that, they can safely locate something that is deep-fried and as far as possible from the words "goat's cheese".

'It takes three reads of a menu to get ordering right: the first to find the sausages; the second to see if there's an interesting alternative; and while your partner is ordering, that last, desperate scan to locate the sausages.

'Never ask what's good: it's all good. And don't ask what they recommend. They'll recommend the leathery old monkfish that they've been trying to shift since Monday. Only have the monkfish if they recommend the sausages.'

CREATING A MENU

In order to create a menu, it is vital that your chef knows and understands these basic principles: understanding produce, understanding combinations, understanding how to cook them and knowing the customer base.

The chef Nico Ladenis, in his *My Gastronomy* cookbook, says that 'perfection is the result of simplicity. That is my philosophy: to be restrained in presentation, to produce each dish consistently and always approaching the ideal.'

His own culinary marriages made in heaven include:

♦ duck and orange;

♦ salmon and sorrel;

♦ strawberries and cream;

♦ steak and chips;

♦ tomatoes and basil;

- chicken with tarragon;

- cold lobster with mayonnaise;

- lamb and garlic;

- fried eggs and bacon;

- foie gras and Sauternes;

- chicken and morels.

I would add steak with a Béarnaise sauce, fish soup with rouille, asparagus with Hollandaise, salmon with a beurre blanc sauce, pork loin with crackling and real apple sauce, lamb with couscous, tiger prawns with Thai ingredients, caviar and chilled vodka. And fish and chips, roast Mediterranean vegetables with goat's cheese, the best cheeses with appropriate bread and wine, bread and butter pudding made with brioche bread and a first class crème anglaise.

Nico's philosophy on food is one of simplicity of approach followed by the use of perfect ingredients. There should be no marriage between meat and shellfish or shellfish and fruit, according to him. Sound principles to go by in my book too. Duck and lobster, duck and papaya, lobster and mango, beef with Cointreau and mango (seen on one menu recently), crab and beef are just some examples which do not sit comfortably together in one dish.

Things that makes a good chef are knowing:

- how to create a simple dish perfectly;

- how to cook a steak or fish faultlessly;

- how to time a dish;

- when to cook each dish to order and in what order.

Garnishing your food

Be wary of over-elaboration. This can be seen by some chefs as adding a touch of sophistication to their dishes. Instead, it adds confusion and totally unnecessary clutter to the plate. What does a slice of orange have to do with a crispy duck and puy lentil salad or a fillet steak? Nothing. Don't even think of over-garnishing. More is less and never more so than on a plate. Food should look like food, not some fanciful concoction.

USING FIRST-RATE PRODUCE

If the chef goes down the route of sourcing second-rate produce it won't taste any better if served on the finest china or the best, whitest linen. A case of the Emperor's Clothes. Nor will expensive carpets or décor help to disguise the fact that the establishment is overcharging for poor food.

A good, honest restaurateur passionate about the business and customers will go out of his or her way to source the best produce around. This does-n't have to mean flying in duck from Paraguay or caviar from the Caspian.

What it means is:

♦ Finding carrots that have flavour and cooking them with interest and knowledge.

♦ Locating a free range chicken that really tastes like chicken and not blotting paper.

♦ Tracking down very well hung beef of note.

♦ Buying good quality chocolate with high cocoa solids for the best chocolate tart.

♦ Finding a herb specialist who will supply French tarragon, not flavour-less Russian tarragon.

♦ Sourcing the basics with understanding and passion: bread, butter, coffee, wine.

A good chef – and the restaurateur who encourages their chefs in the art of finding quality produce – will understand the way to perfection is via superb produce. They will know the culinary job is simply to present these tracked down flavours to the customer.

Don't go looking for difficulty. If certain produce is not available or is tricky to obtain on a regular basis, don't put that dish on the menu. Chefs must have peace of mind when ordering to fulfil a menu's promise.

WHAT TO COOK AND WHY TO COOK IT

Cook what you like eating yourself and you will be halfway there. But if you have a narrow palate you may be in the wrong job! Don't cook what you don't understand. If sauces aren't up your street, but an understanding and pleasure in cooking imaginative vegetarian food is, make this your forte or learn how to cook dishes out of your repertiore.

Women chefs do tend to like cooking food they understand, their raison d'être as a chef often being to give pleasure via the table. It is a huge buzz doing just this to which I and many other women chefs can testify. Many male chefs have the notion that they have to show off. Why?

Alice Waters, the remarkable and much-loved Californian restaurateur who started the trend of looking for the best produce cooked simply (and if she couldn't find it she grew it) is reported to have said:

I opened a restaurant so that people could come and eat; remember that the final goal is to nourish and nurture those who gather at your table. It is there, within this nurturing process, that I have found the greatest satisfaction and sense of accomplishment.

Menu planning and dish creation

Planning the menu is an essential part of eating well. Professional chefs plan their menus with care, taking into account tastes, fashions, trends, health, seasonal food, limitations of time, budget and practicality.

Choosing a wine list to go with your food is equally important. A balanced menu is a must.

When compiling ideas and seeking inspiration ideas for the menu, look first at what you wish to achieve, who you wish to attract to your restaurant, what the kitchen can handle in terms of staff numbers, ability and equipment and the cost to produce each dish.

Many chefs have a germ of an idea in mind when creating new dishes. Talking to people, reading about dishes in the restaurant guides, in newspapers and magazines, seeing dishes created on television by the likes of Gary Rhodes, Rick Stein, Nigella Lawson, Jamie Oliver, Delia Smith *et al* may spark off an idea.

It pays to think each idea through quite thoroughly before putting it on the menu:

♦ How much prepping will this dish require? Can it be costed out favourably enough to put on the menu?

♦ Where do the ingredients come from?

♦ Does it fit in to the existing menu or does it upset the balance of fish, meat, vegetarian and sweet dishes?

Menu balance

Look at whether you now have too many cheese/fish/pork or chicken dishes. Will it look good? Think about whether there are too many same coloured dishes, too many browns and beiges, too many dishes with dairy produce or too many chilli-hot offerings. Is there a lot of fried food, or three types of the ubiquitous salmon?

Nico himself didn't ask this question of balance often enough. One menu of his I recall showed his fondness of offal, customers having to negotiate kidneys, liver, foie gras and sweetbreads with little else on offer. Sometimes even the great ones can get it wrong.

Questions to ask yourself when working out a menu

It can take several years of cooking in a professional kitchen to reach the stage of knowing instinctively what will and what won't work in your kitchen. But don't let the creative process be stilted by fear or indecision. Try out your ideas, present them to your team and ask them.

Or try them out on good customers who will welcome an opportunity to be of use and be flattered by being asked. In the early days of putting a menu together when new to the business, money and time can be wasted. The questions that need answering include:

◆ Is it a worthwhile dish to develop?

◆ Are the ingredients available?

◆ What would my gross profit be on this dish?

◆ Does it keep well or may there be high wastage?

◆ Does it present well?

◆ Can I delegate other chefs to do this dish in my absence or are the skills not present in my current brigade?

You can either change the whole menu at one go or introduce new dishes. As a one-man band (so to speak) I preferred to do the latter as it would have created havoc not only for the kitchen but also with regular customers, who like to see familiar dishes on the menu as well as being offered new ones.

A good chef simply cannot, in my opinion, create dozens of new dishes as perfection, or near-perfection will be lost. Finely tuning a dish takes a while. But, of course, if you are doing an assembly job – putting the best smoked salmon you can find on the menu or oysters or a fine ham with a chicory salad – then little fine tuning is required. The dish can go on the menu right away.

When creating a new menu do also look out for the number of hot and cold starters appearing on it. If you put too many hot ones on, you will slow down the process of getting food out quickly to hungry, impatient customers. Getting that balance right is very important.

MENU AND DRINK PRICING

The aim of pricing is to achieve the best profits and ensure the long-term success of the business. So you need to think about:

♦ What type of customers you will have and what they can pay.

♦ What quality of produce you will buy.

♦ What standards of cooking will be achieved.

♦ What the standards of service and comfort are in the restaurant.

♦ What the competition is like.

♦ What the plans are for the future.

You may wish to keep prices down initially to attract customers and become established. But the danger in this is that your loyal customers, when becoming aware of the price rises, may decamp elsewhere as they can't afford to dine with you. It is an area which needs flair combined with a good business sense.

♦ TOP TIP ♦

Restaurateurs on average should aim to have a 60–70 per cent profit on food and a 60 per cent profit on wines.

CREATE CONTENTED CUSTOMERS

Getting the temperature of the food right is crucial. Do you fiddle about trying to create a tower of jumbled ingredients, the food getting colder by the second? Or do you simply present your food with a quick whisk of cooked food to the plate, dress it minimally if at all, then promptly on to the customer? Avoid having food returned because it is too cold. You will most assuredly have to cook it again from scratch, thereby creating wastage and lowering your gross profit.

Any customer may be slightly anxious, so get that wine, bread and water to them smartly, thereby giving them confidence about your restaurant. These quick acts make them more relaxed.

A rule of thumb in this quick turnaround restaurant business with impatient people is to get the first course out in ten minutes from the order being placed. Fifteen maximum. People may walk out if the half hour is breached. Keep the customer informed if there is a delay. It is appreciated. Offer them more bread, or a free glass of wine to keep them sweet. That is why it is so important to have a good selection of cold starters if the pace of your restaurant is fast.

Be aware too that there is nothing new under the sun when it comes to creating new dishes. It's just reinvention of the culinary wheel but, with top ingredients and good cooking, your food will stand out.

Essential: taste what you put on the menu

Good chefs always taste. One young chef I interviewed for my chefs' column arrogantly told me that he didn't need to taste the food he cooked as he had tasted it once and 'that was enough'. Stuff and nonsense. A good chef always tastes, tastes and tastes. The reason? Your salmon terrine might have a less strong tarragon added so it needs more, you may have not put enough lemon juice or salt and freshly ground pepper in. That ice cream may need more vanilla or coffee, the prawn and coconut dish could do with some more chilli. Could the rouille for the fish soup do with extra garlic?

Good communication between kitchen and front of house

Good chefs always discuss each new dish with waiting staff so that they can talk to the customers with knowledge and be able to sell effectively. If staff just shrug their shoulders or say 'I'll just ask the chef what's in this dish', it will create a bad impression to say the least. There must be harmony and communication between cook and server.

What is your style? Do you have one? Does creativity and ambition show in the cooking? If you do have style do it with conviction. Do things your way and don't copy unless you have the ability to copy well.

The *Automobile's Association Guide's* ten top tips for better restaurant cooking

1. Source your suppliers carefully. Demand the best and only serve the best.

2. Use local produce where possible – if it's good enough.

3. Have one eye on the seasons –although most foods are available all year round, they nevertheless tend to be at their best for only one season.

4. Cook real food from whole raw ingredients.

5. Keep it simple, be true to the ingredients. Don't be creative just for the sake of it.

6. Always question – how can I improve this dish?

7. Taste the food you create. And remember the diner is eating more than just a forkful – so as a plateful, will it be too much, too heavy, too rich, or just plain boring?

8. Keep a sense of balance. Don't overcook, don't undercook, don't over-sauce, don't under-sauce, don't under-season. This sounds really basic, but it's where many meals fail.

9. Eat out. Get to know what the competition's doing.

10. Don't cook for accolades. The best food comes from a kitchen that has confidence in its own ability, where the chef is in tune with the needs of the restaurant's customer base.

MENU WRITING AND COMPILING

As a restaurant critic my heart can sometimes sink when reading a menu and I think 'there is nothing that inspires me here.' Why is this? If the menu is written in flowery language – 'puddles of chive essence', 'a mosaic of', 'a symphony of', multitudes of coulis – it puts me and others off instantly. And what, for heaven's sake, is a 'chef's special'? Something that the kitchen has too much of and is desperate to shift?

It could also be that the balance is decidedly off-putting or the menu itself could be poorly presented. Is it difficult to decipher the-over-the-top hand-writing? I and many others who take a great interest in menus and their readability find the Harvesters of this world and other fast food, so called 'family' restaurants, confusing and very, very long. But by analysing the menu you find that most of the ingredients turn up time and time again under a different guise. Rather like Chinese menus.

- Choose a font that is clear if you are printing the menus in-house.

- Be succinct and clear with your headings.

- State clearly any extras.

- Avoid too many supplements on a *table d' hôte* (set) menu. It might as well be an *à la carte* if they are piled on.

- Tone down the descriptions.

- There is no need to add all the ingredients, as this will confuse. The reader will have to return to many dishes again and again to remind themselves of their contents.

Here is a sample past menu in comic sans font from the Walnut Tree Inn, Monmouthshire, Wales. It is succinct and clear but the balance is some-what questionable.

Walnut Tree Inn

Lunch Menu

TWO COURSES £16.95

THREE COURSES £19.95

STARTERS

Leek and potato soup with pancetta

Salad of endive, pancetta, shaved fennel, dolcelatte and rocket

Home made terrine of wild Welsh rabbit with marrow chutney

Crispy, breadcrumb belly pork with lemon, capers and fennel

MAIN COURSE

Home made venison sausages with mashed potatoes, greens and onion gravy

Home made breadcrumbed fish cake with caesar salad

Braised shoulder of local lamb with rosemary potatoes and greens

Anna's lasagne bolognese

DESSERTS

Home made gelati and sorbetti

Gelati: gianduia, fior de latte, tutti frutti, stacciatella

Sorbetti: blackcurrant, wimberry, pear and saffron

Vanilla pannacotta with bramley apple and raison compote and cinnamon crumble

Panetonne bread and butter pudding

Hot chocolate fondant with praline ice cream

The balance is upset by pancetta in two of the four starters, with more pork in another starter. All four have a meat content. Breadcrumbs are found in two of the eight dishes and more bread comes in the form of bread and butter pudding for dessert.

The majority of dishes are on the heavy, filling side, not in keeping with today's lighter food. The ice creams will need explaining to each customer unless they are Italian-speaking. On the plus side, it does state that the kitchen makes its own food and sources local produce.

Types of menus

There are two types of menu, the ***table d' hôte*** (table of the host), also known more familiarly as the set menu, and the ***à la carte*** (from the card). The key difference between the two is that the ***à la carte*** has differently priced dishes, while the *table d' hôte* has an inclusive price for the whole meal.

The *carte du jour* (literally, card of the day) is not very common these days and offers a fixed meal with one or more courses for a set price. A *prix fixé* (fixed price) menu is similar. Sometimes the price also includes a glass of wine or a substitute drink.

The table d' hôte *menu (set menu)*

◆ A menu with a fixed number of courses.

◆ Limited choice within each course or no choice.

◆ The price is fixed.

◆ The food is usually available at a set time, say between 6–7.30pm.

The à la carte *menu*

◆ The choice is larger than the *table d' hôte*.

◆ Each dish is priced separately.

◆ Each dish is generally cooked to order. Waiting time may be longer.

The advantage for the customer is that there are no hidden charges when ordering the *table d'hôte* or set menu, the disadvantage to that customer is that the portions may be smaller. No bad thing, say some, in this obesity age, but the value for money question may be asked.

The set menu's disadvantage is that the forecasting of how many dishes to prepare isn't straightforward. Too many dishes will lead to wastage. To get around this, keep the food as simple as possible.

For example, add a Roquefort and bacon salad to the starter list rather than a salmon and avocado terrine, as the latter is more in keeping with an *à la carte* menu. The salad is easy and quick to prepare, the wastage minimal.

If you run out of prepared dishes on a set menu, be prepared to offer a more expensive dish with less profit. Therefore, keep the set menu simple, easy to prepare and inexpensive so that all dishes can be quickly and effectively prepped to order.

Tips for menus
To make your menus work:

- Choose ingredients seasonally.

- Choose lighter food for summer and more substantial food for winter including fashionable comfort food.

- Have a good balance of fish, meat, vegetables, cheeses, desserts. For example, have beef, lamb, chicken, offal, fish, vegetarian dishes plus fruit-based, chocolate-based and cream-based desserts.

- Bear in mind that beef is expensive so this may end up as your loss-leader. You will have a better gross profit if staff can steer people towards other dishes.

- Include a selection of plainly cooked food like grilled salmon or a light salad, or be able to offer it should it be asked for.

- Have a balance of hot and cold food.

- Ask staff to introduce customers to more adventurous food on the menu. It may work in a smaller restaurant although it may not be practical in a large one.

- Change the menu not only for the sake of the customer but the chef's too. They mustn't get bored. This is when standards can slip.

- Recognise dishes that don't sell, and remove them from the menu to save wastage and your gross profit falling.

- Your specials board can reflect your buying prowess. If offered some good value, fresh fish by a trusted supplier on the day put it on the specials board, for example.

- Avoid putting on past sell-by-date food on the specials board. Learn to see ahead if some items aren't selling fast enough and then put them on that board. But don't jeopardise your business by trying to off-load going-off food. It's commercial suicide.

- Discuss the menu in detail with the kitchen staff and ask for their input.

- Don't even think about putting something on the menu just because it looks pretty. It has to taste pretty great too.

- Be wary of following fashions. You may end up with a mishmash of dishes that the kitchen can't cope with and are far removed from being the genuine article. Good, authentic sushi is an example.

- Be creative with the trimmings and leftovers. Will fish trimmings make a good fishcake for the specials board, for example? Will cheeses not fit to be seen on the cheese board, due to their miniscule size, be good for stuffing peppers with tomatoes and tapenade as a special?

- You can afford to be ambiguous with something as specialised as game, as availability might suddenly dry up, in which case substitution is the only way forward. 'Game in season served in the traditional way, according to availability' might be an option to write on the menu.

- The advantage of having the menu written up (clearly) on a blackboard menu for a small restaurant is that, if supplies run out of a certain vital ingredient like salmon, you wipe it off the board.

◆ Or if you write the menu on a daily basis if it's a small menu, just don't include the missing dish. That's the joy of being small and impulsive.

◆ If you're not making the margin, the profit, changes have to be made. Ask for prices from another supplier or, if you can, find the same quality from another source by bypassing the middleman.

◆ One method that many chefs use is to add £1 or so on the best-selling dishes. Your profit could be on track again.

SPECIAL DIETS

You will almost certainly have to deal with special diets for people with allergies, who are diabetic, those who wish for a low cholesterol diet or who follow a low salt regime.

Generally speaking, those with medical conditions or who just wish to follow strict eating guidelines will know what they can or can't eat. If the customer explains to a staff member that they are avoiding a particular ingredient it is important for that staff member to find out from the chef if the diner's choice avoids these items. Guessing just won't do.

Allergies
Allergies can include the gluten in wheat, rye and barley. This allergy is known as coeliac. Other allergies can include peanuts and all derivatives, sesame seeds, cashews, pecans, brazils or walnuts, as well as milk, fish, shellfish and eggs.

Diabetic
In those with diabetes, the body is unable to control the level of glucose within the blood. Diets may include avoiding high sugar dishes and some from the cholesterol list below.

Low cholesterol
Avoidance of polyunsaturated fats and limited amounts of animal fats. Food that can be eaten includes lean meat, fish, fruit and vegetables plus low fat milk, cheese and yoghurt.

Low salt (or sodium)
A reduction of salt in the cooking or no salt at all.

Cultural and religious dietary requirements
As our culture becomes more diverse, it may help to be aware of differing requirements by certain faiths and ways of cooking which are allowed.

Muslims
No meat, offal or animal fat unless it is halal meat (as required by Islamic dietary law).

Jews
- No pork or pork products.

- No shellfish.

- No animal fats or gelatine from animals considered to be unclean or not slaughtered according to the prescribed manner.

- Restrictions on methods of preparation and cooking practices.

- Preparation and eating of meat and dairy produce at the same meal is not allowed.

Sikhs
- No beef or pork.

- No halal meat.

- May prefer a vegetarian diet.

Hindhus
- No beef.

- Rarely pork.

- Some Hindhus will not eat any other meats, fish or eggs.

Vegans

◆ No food of any animal origin.

◆ Vegans will eat: vegetables, vegetable oils, cereals, fruits and seeds.

INSTRUCTING KITCHEN STAFF ON FOLLOWING YOUR RECIPES

The head chef is responsible for teaching staff how to cook recipes devised by him or her in an abbreviated, professional way. These recipes are a kind of shorthand, a checklist of ingredients and method, a variety of pointers rather than the usual recipe of full measurements found in cookbooks.

Develop a card system or file away recipes on a computer. Then you can always find the required recipe at short notice to give it to a new chef who may not have cooked the dish before or is not familiar with your method.

Compile a master file in which each recipe is under headings such as soups (hot and cold), salads (warm and cold), chicken, fish, beef, lamb, liver and so on.

For desserts you could have sub-headings such as ice creams, English puddings, fruit tarts, dairy desserts, pastries and basic preparations such as proper custard and chocolate sauce.

Add the date when the dish was on the menu, where the original recipe came from, its page if from a cookbook. Cross-indexing is also helpful, eg lemon-based recipes.

Add notes to recipes too if they have been modified, such as that the temperature needed to be changed, the type of chocolate giving the best results, how many servings each recipe yields.

For ease of teaching, stick to either the metric or imperial system. This will simplify the work in the kitchen, with everyone on the same wavelength at least measurement-wise.

Example of long recipe and its shortened version

Apple tart on puff pastry with a caramel sauce: for two

4 golden delicious dessert apples, peeled, halved and cored

2 thin rounds of puff pastry 15 cm in diameter and pricked with a fork to prevent rising

10 g caster sugar

knob of butter

sugar syrup (see recipe card)

caramel sauce (see recipe card)

1. Pre-heat the oven to 170 c. Cut the apples into very thin slices and arrange around the pastry in a circle, starting at the edge and working towards the centre.

2. Sprinkle the apples with sugar then dot with the butter.

3. Place the tarts on a baking tray and bake for around 10–15 minutes or until the base is cooked and light brown. If the apples have not caramelised well place under a grill or salamander, covering the edges of the pastry so that they don't burn. Or use a blow torch.

4. Glaze with the sugar syrup and serve with several tablespoonfuls of caramel sauce.

The reduced version

Apple tart recipe: for two

4 apples, peeled, cored and cut thinly

2 rounds of puff pastry

caster sugar

butter

sugar syrup (see recipe card)

caramel sauce (see recipe card)

Put apple slices on pastry in circles, sprinkle with sugar, add butter. Bake in 170 c oven until browned and caramelised. Continue with blow torch if necessary. Glaze with sugar syrup. Garnish with caramel sauce.

10

Choosing Suppliers

A chef, no matter how brilliant, will not be able to metaphorically pull the rabbit from the hat if the produce sourced is cheap and nasty. As food is increasingly simply prepared rather than sauced, casseroled, stewed or prepared in a more complex way, the ingredients are given centre stage. No hiding behind a blanket of rich cream sauce over horridly sourced chicken. **Your food will be judged on its quality**.

Therefore, choose your suppliers with the utmost care. Work out your gross profit with quality at the forefront of all your calculations. Search for excellent meat, a good supplier of game and fish, top notch vegetables and fruit. Don't even think of skimping on quality cheeses, eggs, smoked foods, coffee, chocolates. Or anything. Not even the salt and pepper you cook with and place on the table.

HOW TO LOOK FOR KEY SUPPLIERS

Your bread is vital to get right. This sets the tone as it may be the first mouthful a customer has in your restaurant. And as for dried goods, olive oils, olives and all manner of specialist foods, there is a plethora of suppliers now in Britain and Ireland. Or import directly from a company abroad. Go to food fairs, events, exhibitions locally, regionally and in major cities to track down the best produce.

Taste. Taste. Taste. If you have a good chutney at a restaurant, some excellent cheese, a smoked duck to die for, ask how to find these suppliers. Talk to other restaurateurs, the generous-hearted ones will be only too willing to pass on good suppliers to you. And the ones to avoid.

Get price lists. Ask for samples. Bargain. Ask for wholesale prices. Consider buying by mail order. As a restaurant consultant employed to set up restaurant kitchens, I go to as many exhibitions as possible. I can find the best quality food around, taking into account what the restaurant's aims are and its pricing structure, as well as using other methods of sourcing.

I keep an eye out in delicatessens and take down the company's name for products I wish to sample. Consult the *Yellow Pages* for other sources, go on the web to locate cheese companies and other specialist companies. Cross the channel to buy more cheaply if you're in the south of England. But always think quality. Always ask to taste anything before buying. It's quite normal in France!

If you can, visit Borough Market, Borough Street, London, SE1 near London Bridge (0207) 407 1002 for a shortcut to finding superb produce.

Contact Covent Garden Market in London and other major fruit and vegetable markets in your area for suppliers.

Working with your suppliers

Once you have narrowed down your suppliers and start buying from them, always check your supplies, throw anything back at them that doesn't have quality stamped all over it (in the nicest possible way of course) and establish an excellent working rapport with them. This way they will look after you and will bend over backwards to keep your business. Always promptly query any accounting error and pay your bills on time.

◆ TOP TIP ◆
You are not joined at the hip with your suppliers. Continue to locate even better ones.

Suppliers will usually call you to find out what your order is. Or call them. There is usually an after-hours ordering service to leave messages on for next day delivery.

Tips for buying.

◆ Fish is selling fast these days. Always but always have the freshest fish. Once it's past its best, toss it. Or be prepared to lose a customer.

◆ Game is gaining momentum thanks to its healthy eating tag. There is wild and farmed game and do try boar on your menu.

◆ Demand longer hanging for your beef from your supplier, 28 days or over. Nothing less. Look out for darker coloured, marbled meat.

◆ Insist on the best vegetables for intense flavour. Go organic for tastier vegetables. Try different varieties. There's more to life than carrots.

◆ Fruit: it is worth doing some research to find really tasty fruit, apples in particular. Woolly peaches, dull apples and strawberries abound.

◆ Find a good cheese supplier – or three. Shop around for regional cheeses.

◆ Make sure your staff can identify the cheeses when serving them.

◆ There is some truly awful smoked salmon out there. Be discerning.

◆ Don't buy just any chocolate. Source one with high cocoa solids.

◆ Coffee finishes off a good meal with character. Make sure yours is memorable. Source the best and invest in an espresso machine.

KITCHEN SUPPLIES AND SUPPLIERS

When I started as chef/restaurateur of Soanes, Petworth, West Sussex, in the 1980s, local produce sourcing was extremely limited. Excellent fish, vegetables and cheeses had to come from Covent Garden or Rungis, the Paris market.

Only the local butcher and a mushroom forager offered goods I was seeking. I grew herbs and some vegetables and salads. Local wholesale suppliers could only offer second-class vegetables and fruit, dull, tasteless salads, even poorer tomatoes. The couldn't care less attitude was deeply dispiriting, hence the long-distance sourcing.

What is possible to source

Today's restaurateurs are spoilt for choice if they wish to source quality ingredients which are local, regional and seasonal. The added advantage is that this helps to cut food miles and, as a result, pollution and fuel consumption. But do restaurateurs source locally?

The omens are promising. There is a stealthy trend for the better restaurateurs to offer locally or regionally sourced sausages, cheeses, meat, vegetables, fruit and drink to their customers. They prefer to know the provenance of their supplies. But does the quality shine, is the produce chosen with knowledge? Perhaps the buying of local and regional food is merely paying lip service to trends.

Does the customer really know or mind? Or worse still are they unable to tell the difference between a carrot grown with care around the corner and a mass-produced Dutch or British hothouse one? Our tastebuds, having been assaulted by over-processed food for years, could be immune to quality now that large servings of cheap food are the consumer yardstick.

There does however seem to be a growing band of customers with heightened expectations, resulting in the raising of standards by local and regional producers. They relish the difference and vote with their feet, choosing restaurants and pubs that celebrate the 'extra mile' travelled by the chef to source the best food around without the stabilisers, additives and other 'benefits' of mass-produced food.

WHAT SOME CHEFS AND RESTAURATEURS WANT AND ACHIEVE

As multi-restaurant owner Sir Terence Conran said at a star-studded gathering of chefs at the Manoir Aux Quat' Saisons' (Raymond Blanc's hotel/restaurant in Oxfordshire) American Food Revolution debate I attended in 2004, 'I want to eat the cuisine of the country, democratic food. I am passionately interested in the improvement of quality ingredients cooked simply.'

Alice Waters, chef/owner of Chez Panisse in California, also spoke at the debate. For over three decades she has developed a 60-strong network of mostly local farmers and ranchers whose dedication to sustainable agriculture assures her restaurant of a steady supply of fresh ingredients. Her set menu format is based purely on seasonal produce.

This iconic chef, basing her commitment on French practices she witnessed on sabbatical in France after university, chose this non-compromising ethic right from the start: not to depend on unreliable quality and inconsistencies from commercial food wholesalers. Try to get a table at Chez Panisse.

Conran's and Waters' passion for this 'democratic' food is filtering through as a growing band of chefs and restaurateurs realise the untold benefits to their business when sourcing the best produce in the region.

The importance of sourcing

Look at food on menus at restaurants listed in *The Good Food Guide* and other comprehensive guides and you will notice – if you haven't already – an increase in provenance: Lincolnshire grey partridge, Goosenargh and Deben duck, Cumbrian fell-bred meat, Cotswolds, Nidderdale, Southdown, Wiltshire and organic Highgrove lamb, Dales-bred beef smoked and cured in Yorkshire ale.

Rare-breed well-hung beef such as Longhorn rump and Black Welsh fillet from butchers are accredited by the Rare Breeds Survival Trust. The ingredients are allowed to speak for themselves with minimal cooking and a return to simplicity.

Fish too is much sought-after. Mindful restaurateurs source eco-friendly fish from Cornwall and Devon, Cromer crab and Skye scallops. Local and regional cheeses are another growing commodity on this carefully chosen route.

Prime examples

Weaver's Shed restaurant in West Yorkshire goes one step further. They produce their own chicken, duck, quails' eggs and vegetables. Co-chef, co-owner Stephen Jackson's father, a retired CEO of a major company, grows cavolo nero, kholrabi, leeks, salads, soft fruits and no less than 75 herbs and wild plants for the transformed woollen mill. The saving, Stephen reckons, is £200 a week off the supplier bill, 'a sensible way of progressing and cooking within the seasons.'

Lawrence Murphy, chef/owner of Fat Olives in Emsworth, Hampshire, a brasserie-style restaurant, 'gets local rabbit and game and two guys fish for sea bass in the Solent for us.' The menu reflects this enthusiastic, innovative chef's local food, with sourcing that includes all vegetables and fruit in season.

The Star Inn at Harome, North Yorkshire, is a showcase of English-sourced food with most dishes markedly quoting the provenance. Yoadwarth Mill salmon, Whitby crab, North Sea lobster, Pickering watercress, Sand Hutton asparagus, Ryedale lamb, local fallow deer, Yorkshire Blue cheese are just some of the goods sourced by chef Andrew Pern, winner of many accolades thanks to his diligence.

Of farming stock, Andrew is in the Alice Waters mould, sourcing seasonal produce within his own village, the Dexters bred for the table in view of the restaurant. Gloucester Old Spots are being reared in a nearby orchard on apples and 'everybody takes pride in their produce.' The network includes honey and duck eggs, also from Harome, and olive oils from Carluccio's.

'We've set the benchmark in the area with healthy competition from other pubs and restaurants upping the game,' Andrew adds. 'It's in everyone's interests.' The facts speak for themselves: over 1,000 people eat here a week.

At the other end of the sourcing scale comes Peter Gordon, the New Zealand co-chef/co-owner of London's Providores, a restaurant of fusions. 'I treat the world's culinary resources as one huge and exciting larder,' Peter says.

The restaurant and café's eclectic menu covers a huge range from Exmoor-sourced duck, New Zealand venison and Suffolk Cross lamb to pomegranate molasses ('now available here thanks to its exposure'), plan-tains, tomatillos, jicama, yuzu, wasabi tobiko, jeijoa and kirmizi biber and Turkish chilli flakes 'usually brought over from a friend in Turkey.' Waiting staff must spend a lot of time explaining what the ingredients are. Cheeses are specifically British, other ingredients sourced from specialist suppliers.

SOURCING ALTERNATIVES

The alternatives to local food sourcing are supermarkets (for smaller restaurants), local wholesale and retail, cash and carry, specialist food com-panies and farmers' markets.

How not to source your food

There are many national wholesale suppliers like Brakes (formerly Brake Bros) whose lorries criss-cross Britain and France, their buying power and market dominance creating an astonishing £1.4 billion annual turnover.

There is no need for chefs to do any cooking whatsoever if sourcing Brake products. Cocktail BBQ chicken drumlettes, Brake crinkle cut fries, and peach and champagne tart were all medal winners at the 2003 British Frozen Food Federation Annual Awards.

The major supplier of frozen, chilled and ambient foods to the trade including J.D. Wetherspoons across the UK, Brakes' corporate message is a chilling one. 'Consumer and market trends', 'product assessment', 'total solution provider', 'customer to really focus on … developing their branded estate', 'cost controls', 'pouch, c-pet tray or multi-portion foil' packaging, with nary a foray into selling food with passion, or indeed a regional or local slant.

Readymade soups, boeuf bourguionne (sic), mashed potato or salmon mousse to free up the 'busy chef' for executive paperwork – Brakes' recipes are all part of the service.

Witness Baked Garlic Chicken and Pancake Tagliatelle, cited product numbers given: 'simply thaw one Chicken Supreme (3042) and smother in garlic and herb cream cheese. Wrap in two rashers of thawed Beechwood Smoked Back Bacon (2806) and pan fry in 5g butter for seven minutes each side.' Then you're asked to toss in Chopped Garlic (4017), shredded French Butter Crepes (3160) and Mange Tout (4741) in some more butter. Sprinkle with Finely Chopped Parsley (4019).

Voilà! You are a chef! No need to get down and dirty by doing the leg work in good food sourcing or real cooking, let alone think.

3663 ('spells food on your keyboard') is another nationwide wholesale company whose sales are also over £1 billion a year. It offers frozen and chilled food delivered by 1,000 vehicles to over 50,000 customers in the catering trade, including Pret à Manger. Their 600-strong Smart Choice range includes ready meals, sauces, soups, canned produce and ice creams. Sales are booming. Think of those food miles by both companies. Think of the quality.

FOOD FOR THOUGHT

The less we know of food via family, home economics, school meals and eating meals in a social setting, and where food comes from, how it is grown, reared and produced, the less good, well-sourced food will matter.

If this is the public mindset of the future, hard-working, caring, responsible restaurants may be fighting a losing battle to move sourcing to an altogether higher level of quality. Good produce and skilful cooking may mean little to the next generation of chefs – and customers.

Raymond Blanc, chef/owner of the Manoir Aux Quat' Saisons and instigator of the six-day American Revolution debate, contributes 'that British chefs desperately need to sharpen up. They're not connected with their food.'

He adds: 'How can we encourage the UK to move from cheap food to "real food"? This applies to everyone's food, not just in the restaurant trade.'

The British Protected Food Names Scheme

The EU Protected Food Names Scheme, a British version of the *appellation controlée* system that exists in France to safeguard their wines, has been in operation for 11 years, with Cornish clotted cream and Jersey Royal potatoes as prime examples. PFNS' *raison d'être* is to protect regional and traditional foods whose authenticity and origin can be guaranteed through independent inspection. But who is aware of PFNS?

Sourcing food from Britain and abroad

There is no doubt that eating out is even more pleasurable knowing where the food on our plates comes from, be it regional or local. Or, indeed, whether the olive oil or balsamic vinegar has been derived with passion and erudition from abroad.

Obviously not all produce can come from this country. The best foie gras, black pudding, cured hams like Parma, specialist cheeses, pistachios, limes, lentils and most wines are just a trickle of global riches to our shores.

The Slow Food Movement

Carlo Petrini, president of Slow Food, the 18 year-old association that was formed to defend Italian regional foods and is now an international movement with 80,000 members, declares that 'a gastronome who isn't an environmentalist is a fool'. He adds that people must know where food comes from and how it's produced.

The association protects traditional foods at risk of extinction in many countries and safeguards breeds of animals, wines, pulses, vegetables, fruits, cheeses, cured meat and fish. Website: www.slowfood.com

QUALITY AND PROVENANCE OF PRODUCE

Do we care enough as consumers? We have a vested interest in helping beleaguered farmers who look for alternatives in keeping their farms afloat, their animals' welfare and the quality of all yields at the top of the agenda. But only if they can come up with the goods, not for nostalgia or purely for loyalty. The produce has to stand out.

The same applies to all produce in this new marketplace of small suppliers where taste and quality must be the foremost criteria. Since 1979, UK growers' produce has dwindled to supplying just four per cent of fruit and 52 per cent of the vegetables we eat. Mangetouts from Peru travel 6,312 miles, green beans from southern Africa 5,979 miles.

Polytunnels

Polytunnels, those industrialised structural eyesores, now produce up to 80 per cent of summer fruit. Five thousand acres of Herefordshire, Kent and Scotland alone are now pastures of plastic. The season has been extended by months thanks to this method of growing. Just down the road from me is Tangmere airfield, part of the Battle of Britain strategy and now one of Europe's largest pepper nurseries with over 50 acres of glasshouses on its 115 acres of land.

Salads, herbs, vegetables, flowers and ingredients, previously more likely to have been flown in from other parts of the world are now grown in poly-tunnels. The defence from growers is that 'it is British, good for local economy and we should be proud' despite a desecration of the landscape.

The growth of polytunnels is largely due to supermarkets which demand reliable, unblemished fruit and vegetables. Ethnic restaurant chefs benefit from being able to source some of their produce such as pak choy. However, the quality and variety are not good according to restaurants like Nahm, the London Thai restaurant, which has to import its fernleaf, turmeric, lemongrass and other ingredients directly from Bangkok K Martin & Son, small Lincolnshire producers, supply Indian restaurants with specialist herbs including methi (fenugreek) from their polytunnels.

The *Guardian* newspaper gardener, Monty Don, mounted a campaign with others against strawberries, 'tasteless junk fruit', grown in 250 acres of 'ugly polytunnels' near his Herefordshire home when the company S & A

Davies began building an 18-acre labour camp of 300 mobile homes and amenity centre. And won.

He, I and countless others query the quality of produce grown in these poly-tunnels, the scarring of the landscape and the misuse of migrant workers.

Having vision

If only I and other restaurateurs in the 1980s had had the courage and vision of Alice Waters and others like her to encourage local suppliers when sourcing food. We should demand food that tastes of something rather than the current British strawberry, which is 'helped' along by 17 fungicides and 16 insecticides and still tastes of nothing.

Nearly 20 years on there is much to celebrate but we, as customers, chefs and restaurateurs, need to keep the pressure on or vote with our feet for a greener, more sustainable, definitely tastier Britain.

USEFUL CONTACTS FOR SOURCING PRODUCE

Government agencies are included in this list. There are plenty of other producers to discover. Consult the *Yellow Pages*, your local council and websites via Google or others.

◆ TOP TIP ◆

Just one word of warning: just because it's local doesn't necessarily mean it's good. Be choosy! Locate the best produce possible and help raise standards.

Chef suppliers directory (*Hotelkeeper & Caterer*): (0208) 62 4700 or email chotsen@rbi.co.uk

National and government agencies

National Association of Farmers' Markets: www.farmersmarkets.net

DEFRA (Department of Environment, Food and Rural Affairs): (0207) 238 6687

Department of Agriculture and Rural Development (Northern Ireland): www.dardni.gov.uk

Regional

Buckinghamshire Food Group: (01296) 383345 env-edt@bucksscc.gov.uk

East Anglian Fine Foods: www.foodanddrinkforum.co.uk

East Midlands Fine Foods: www.eastmidlandsfinefood.co.uk

Food From Britain: www.foodfrombritain.com

Guild of Fine Food Retailers: wwwfinefoodworld.co.uk

Hampshire Fare: www.hampshirefare.co.uk

Heart of England Fine Foods: www.heff.co.uk

Henrietta Green's Food Lovers' Club: www.foodloversbritain.com

Highland and Islands Enterprise: www.scottishfoodanddrink.com

Kentish Fare: www.kentishfare.co.uk

Local producers: www.buylocalfood.co.uk

London Food Link: www.londonfoodlink.org

North West Fine Foods: www.nw-fine-foods.co.uk

Northumbria Larder: www.northumbria-larder.co.uk

Oxfordshire Food Group: (01865) 484116 localfood@brookes.ac.uk

South East Food Group Partnership: www.buylocalfood.co.uk

A Taste of Sussex at Sussex Enterprise: www.sussexenterprise.co.uk

Taste of the West: www.tasteofthewest.co.uk

Scottish Enterprise: www.scottishfoodanddrink.com

Scottish Food and Drink: (0141) 228 2409

Scottish Organic Producers Association: www.sopa.org.uk

A Taste of Ulster: (0289) 0665630

Tastes of Anglia: www.tastesofanglia.com

Wales: The True Taste: www.walesthetruetaste.com or 08457 775577

Welsh Development Agency: www.foodwales.co.uk

Welsh Organic Meat: www.cambrianorganics.com

Yorkshire Regional Food Group: www.yorkshireregionalfoodgroup.co.uk

Specialists

British Cheese Board: www.britishcheese.com

The British Herb Association: (0207) 331 7415

British Sheep Dairying Association: BSDA@btopenworld.com

The Chocolate Society: www.chocolate.co.uk

Culinary Events Ltd: events@thecheeseweb.com

Fairtrade Foundation: www.fairtrade.org.uk

The Garlic Information Centre: (01424) 892440

Specialist Cheesemakers Association: www.specialistcheesemakers.co.uk

Ethnic food companies and associations

There are many more to choose from locally and nationally. Many supply via mail order.

Chinese and Asian Foods: Wing Yip: (0208) 450 0422

Japanese: Yaohan Oriental Shopping Centre: (0208) 200 0009

Indian ingredients: Patel Brothers: (0208) 672 2792

Italian ingredients: I Camisa and Son: (0207) 437 7610

Mexican ingredients: The Cool Chile Company: (0870) 902 1145

Moroccan ingredients: Le Maroc: (0208) 968 9783

Spanish ingredients: R Garcia and Sons: (0207) 221 6119

11

Wine and Other Drinks

Wine is one of the more misunderstood subjects for the would-be restaurateur. They need to know what to buy, how to buy it, how to price it and sell it.

This chapter deals with:

- ◆ wines;
- ◆ wine buying;
- ◆ storage;
- ◆ guidance for compiling a wine list;
- ◆ serving wine;

- how to deal with corked bottles;

- wine and food and types of wine with food.

Wine diversity, a global market of wines from across the world, is also discussed and there is a helpful wine vocabulary list. Trading Standards guidelines for alcoholic weights and measurements are featured too.

Coffee, tea and water are also covered in this chapter, this trinity being equally important to get right.

GETTING WINES RIGHT

Jake Watkins, chef/proprietor of JSW in Petersfield, Hampshire has no less than 800 wines stored underneath his small bar floor, accessible only by a hatch. Does he have a large restaurant? No. JSW seats a mere 22.

A highly knowledgeable and enthusiastic exponent of wine and food, Michelin star holder, Jake is perhaps an exception to the rule in the restaurant trade. He has both food and wine hats firmly on.

Jake specialises in German white wines and has a serious collection of them. But it is a finely tuned, well-balanced wine list with plenty of good-value bottles from major European and New World regions. He sensibly also offers eight wines by the glass. And well chosen they are too. Not any old plonk as favoured by many a restaurateur.

The choice of wines is of paramount importance. To be a serious contender for a good, lengthy wine list you have to have enough storage space. You have to have enough knowledge to source wines to match your menu. Consider how much importance you attach to wine in your restaurant first of all. Does it have a role at all? Obviously, if you're opening a small café with no licence then it is of little interest. The coffee is the important selling point here.

But for all other would-be restaurateurs it is vital to get wines right for your operation. This is how you achieve it.

Tips for wine buying and storage:

- First, sort out your storage. How much space do you have?

- Cellars are perfect for wine storage as they keep the wines at a constant cool temperature and the corks don't dry out.

- Wine doesn't like wildly fluctuating temperatures, vibration or warmth.

- Start with a small list as tying money up in wines can be costly.

- Seek the advice of a wine consultant, or perhaps approach a wine writer if unsure yourself of how to put a list together.

- Wine consultants can provide a short cut to reputable suppliers who can supply wines on a consistent basis.

- Wine consultants and wine writers have a great knowledge of the trade and attend many wine tastings. They are generally freelance and are therefore subjective rather than tied to a particular supplier or producer.

- Do you go for a safe, less than exciting list or do you take chances selling less well known wines?

- A good supplier will hold tastings for you and your staff. They will keep cases in storage for you, with the wines kept at the right temperature too.

- A good supplier will go through the menu with you and marry wines with the food.

- The older wines get, the more carefully they need to be treated.

THE DIVERSE WINE LIST

Gone are the days when French wine dominated the wine list. Wines from Australia, New Zealand, South Africa, Chile, Argentina, Spain, Italy and, to a lesser extent, the USA, Germany and Eastern Europe are chosen thanks to the growth of wine retailing and, of course, the vast improvements in wine making. Canada's British Columbia wines are a case in point. Don't dismiss other countries' wines just because they may be unknown to you. The Lebanon, for example, has a long history in good wine-making.

Restaurant wine lists have gone in search of wines to match the diversity of the global food that is now on our menus. As a result previously unknown grapes such as the spicy, fleshy viognier, the musky, aromatic pinot gris, the plummy voluptuous merlot and the rich shiraz are happily commonplace.

Go beyond the chardonnays of this world. They have dominated the market for far too long and are seen as a desperately over-oaked cliché unless terrific ones have been sourced by the restaurateur.

Wines for the restaurant:

- Choose good house wines, not poor quality ones.

- Not everyone likes chardonnay, especially over-oaked ones.

- Choose several house wines of differing grapes: sauvignon blanc, semillon, chenin blanc, viognier, cabernet sauvignon, shiraz, merlot, tempranillo and zinfandel are just a few to choose from.

- Most inexpensive and medium-priced wines are meant to be drunk immediately, i.e not stored for future drinking.

- Have a good number of wines by the glass, not just one.

- Another popular way of selling wines is by the 50 centilitre or litre decanter and it gives an extended feeling of informality.

- Have a wide-ranging list, however small, and not just the ones favoured by the restaurateur as it may not be broad enough for customers' own tastes.

- Avoid well-known supermarket wines. Customers know their price and may be appalled by the mark-up.

- Don't palm the kitchen off with inferior wines to cook with. The poor quality will regrettably shine through.

- Heading grape types with minimal information on the list is a help for customers who may not understand the differing grape tastes.

- The cooler the climate, the leaner the wine. The alcohol percentage can be as low as 9–11 per cent.

- In hotter climates, wines will have tropical fruit flavours, many having a robust 14 per cent alcohol.

- Promote wines well, with information on tables, by the bar and in the window menu site.

◆ TOP TIP ◆

Wine storage temperatures

Wine should be stored in a dark, secure, ventilation-free area which can be locked.

Red wine should be stored at 14c–16c and white wine at 10c–12c.

Wording on the wine list

Keep it simple. Phrases and words like 'excellent length' and 'cigar box aromas' are best avoided for the average restaurant. The mention of vintages and premiers crus (first growths) are equally an alienating minefield for those customers with a shaky knowledge of wines.

You don't want to put your customers off buying a bottle. So make the wine list headings accessible, like 'wines under £12', 'wines under £20'. Or go for the 'light bodied', 'medium bodied', full bodied' which gives the customer instant access. Your wine list could have headings like mellow, spicy, dry or sweet for even greater simplicity.

It helps sales considerably to keep not only the wording simple but also the headings. But entice the reader with your descriptions if using them. Be concise and enthusiastic. Avoid pomposity.

Of course, wording such as 'aromas of blackberry fruit,' 'oaky earthiness' and 'ripe cherry fruit' can all conjure up an instant picture, but be aware of going down the totally over the top descriptive route. It has two disadvantages: it creates customer confusion and it may highlight a poor understanding of wine by the restaurateur which doesn't inspire confidence.

Naturally, if your restaurant is more upmarket, and your projected wine list is a much more serious one with vintages and bristling with big name wines, you might wish to enlist the help of a wine writer or supplier with the wording. But be as succinct as possible, particularly if the list is a long one.

There is no need to put the alcoholic content of each wine on the list but it may be appreciated as it can give an indication to those who prefer a less robust wine – or vice versa.

Tips for serving wine:

◆ Choose glasses that complement wine. Don't even think of serving wine, no matter how inexpensive the wine is, in Paris goblets as you've barely tasted or smelt the wine before swallowing it.

◆ Choose instead a plain, clear glass with a generously sized bowl that tapers slightly before the rim. The stem should be long enough for the glass to be held by the stem, not the bowl, as body warmth will heat up the wine.

◆ Clean glasses properly, making sure that there is no washing liquid residue on the rim as this will destroy the taste of any wine.

◆ Glasses need to be stored bowl up, not stem up, to stop trapping stale air.

◆ Chill white wines, but not too much, as this can dull their aroma and flavour.

◆ Red wines can be over-warmed in a warm restaurant so take care where you store them, i.e. not near radiators, in a hot kitchen, in the bar by the coffee machine or by bright lights.

◆ There is no need to pull the cork on wines an hour ahead of drinking. The majority of wines these days don't really need opening up, as they did in the past when reds were likely to be tough and tannic.

◆ Restaurateurs need to be able to talk with a degree of knowledge to customers about wine in general and their wine list in particular.

◆ Staff should know about wine. Get them tasting. Make up notes for each wine to give to staff.

♦ When serving wine, staff should always present the bottle to the customer before opening it.

♦ Train staff to open a bottle properly by cutting the foil and removing the cork. Never ever try to extract a stubborn cork by placing the bottle between the knees and yanking it out.

♦ Train staff to pour wine only half to two-thirds full in the glass, so that your customers can enjoy the aroma, leaving room to swirl the wine around the glass.

♦ Customers increasingly like to be in control of their wine. The constant topping up by waiting staff in order to sell more wine is not acceptable, it is a hard-sell tactic which is not appreciated and the customer may not return.

♦ Always store wines on their sides, never upright.

Corked and other undrinkable wine

♦ Corked wine: a musty, dank smell caused by cork contamination. Replace.

♦ White wine with a sherry smell and usually with a dark yellow colour has been oxidised (too much air via the cork).

♦ Bad egg or drain smell indicates too much sulphur in the wine.

♦ Thin, sharp wine may not be to everyone's taste, but if it's sour then it shouldn't be served.

♦ Stewed, baked, rather flabby red wine usually means over fermentation. Nor should this be served.

♦ Return all corked or tainted wine to your suppliers.

WINE AND FOOD

Traditionally, white wine went with fish, red with meat. In Britain today, with its less strong food culture, and in contrast to Europe where food has changed little in comparison, we have borrowed extensively from the globe.

As a result, the guide book has been jettisoned. There are no hard and fast rules and no dire combinations that set the teeth on edge. You may argue that plainly cooked fish isn't suited to a robust tannic red, but serve it with a fruity light red and it is a successful marriage.

◆ TOP TIP ◆

Most meals benefit from having a lighter wine first then a fuller-bodied one, a drier wine before a sweeter one, a younger wine before a vintage one. Raw, steamed and poached food is more suited to a light wine, robust wines going better with roasts and chargrills.

Choosing wines to suit a whole table who have all chosen different dishes can prove problematical. A wine that will go with the majority is an answer, or choices by the glass for each individual.

Dessert wines

Dessert wines are fast growing in popularity. Chill well and serve them in small glasses. Once opened, dessert wines will keep for longer than other wines. Look beyond the ubiquitous Muscat de Beaumes de Venise. The choice is sensational. And good for profit margins. Add several types of dessert wines by the glass to your dessert menu.

Types of wine with food

A general guide but, as mentioned, the rules are here to be broken:

Crisp, dry, fresh whites: salads, chicken and fish.

Smooth, medium-bodied whites: pasta, creamy sauces, chicken, salmon.

Full-bodied, rich whites: lobster, turbot, slightly spicy style of Pacific Rim cooking.

Aromatic and medium-dry whites: Riesling with spicy Thai food, Gewurztraminer with Chinese, Tokay-Pinot Gris with foie gras.

Rosé: making a comeback. Good with sharply dressed salads and summer food.

Light, fruity reds: pasta, pizzas, chicken, vegetarian dishes.

Smooth, medium-bodied reds: almost anything, French ones more suited to classic French dishes.

Full-bodied reds: beef, game, casseroles and cold weather food. An enthusiast's wine.

Champagne and sparkling wines: surprisingly versatile. A richer, fuller-flavoured champagne can be drunk throughout a meal but try demi-sec champagne with fruit-based desserts as dry champagne with a rich dessert doesn't work too well.

Dessert wines: pure nectar. Muscats and sweet Bordeaux go well with apple, pear and peach desserts. Australian liqueur muscats partner chocolate with dash. Mavrodaphne of Patras, a red Greek dessert wine, matches chocolate too.

♦ TOP TIP ♦

People go first of all for the wine price, then the country of origin and then the grape.

PRICING WINE

Customers take issue with the high mark up of wines, especially if they recognise the wine that they can buy in a supermarket or a high street wine merchant's and know full well the retail cost. The next thought that occurs to customers is the wholesale price to the restaurant, i.e. the even lower price paid by the restaurateur, and the resentment builds.

But, as Alistair Gibson of the Brookfield Hotel and Hermitage restaurant in Emsworth, Hampshire – and a wine merchant too – rightly states, retailers just have to buy in the wines and put them on the shelves. Their profit per bottle is around 28 per cent.

A restaurateur offers an experience, waiting staff, glasses, the cleaning of those glasses, a chair, table, perhaps music. All of this has to be paid for on top of the rent, rates, insurance and all the other expenses that go with running a restaurant. There is also the money wrapped up in stock and keeping the wines in a good condition.

Therefore, a profit of 60 per cent is the average for house wines. The other wines on that all-important list will be on a profit sliding scale. However, it is better to have those wines shifting than gathering dust, so offer a 'specials board' of wines by the glass or bottle.

WINE VOCABULARY

AOC: *appellation d'origine controlée*, created by French authorities to establish specific areas of production, grape varieties and which also covers maximum yield per hectare, sugar and alcohol, pruning of the vine, cultivation and wine making methods.

Alcohol: an essential element in wine, alcohol is produced when enzymes created by yeasts change the sugar content of the grape juice into alcohol, carbon dioxide and heat.

Aroma: the wine's scent defined by the type of grape(s), fermentation and the age of the wine. The bouquet.

Barrel fermented: wine that is fermented in oak barrels rather than stainless steel tanks.

Blanc de blancs: literally 'white of whites', a white wine made with white grapes like a champagne from chardonnay grapes.

Blanc de noirs: white wine made from black grapes.

Blending: also known as assemblage, the mixing of types of wine varieties to make a more balanced wine. Bordeaux wines are usually a blend of cabernet sauvignon, cabernet franc and merlot fermented grapes.

Body: a wine with good tannic structure and good ageing potential.

Botrytis: a mould that attacks grapes either as grey rot which may endanger the harvest or as noble rot, used to make luscious dessert wines such as Sauternes and the Hungarian Tokaji.

Claret: the British name for Bordeaux red wines.

Cru: literally, from French, a growth. It dates back to 1855 to denote a vineyard's rank in Bordeaux which then divided into five classes or crus.

Cuvée: literally, a vatful.

Decanting: the separating of the sediment of a wine. Decanting from the bottle to a glass container adds more oxygen to the wine to make it more palatable. If the wine is old, it can be a disaster as it can mean a quicker deterioration.

Fermentation, alcoholic: transformation of the sugar in the must into alcohol and carbon dioxide in the presence of yeast.

Fortified: a wine which has had wine spirit (brandy) added to it, like port or sherry.

Kabinett: high-quality German wines.

Must: unfermented grape juice obtained by crushing or pressing.

NV: non-vintage.

Oxidised wine: sherry-like or nutty flavour caused by the action of oxygen on wine due mainly to exposure to air, heat and light.

Reserve: for special cuvées (vats) set aside for ageing or for future use. It also refers to a minimum ageing period for certain spirits like Calvados, Cognac or Armagnac.

Sec, secco, seco: dry in French, Italian and Portuguese or Spanish.

Spatlese: late-harvested German wines.

Tannin: different types of tannins created by the stalks, pips and skins from grapes plus nuts, wood bark and berries which are released during the fermentation process and the pressing. These tannins give the wine its specific character and contribute to its ageing. Wine storage in new wood allows extra tannins to be absorbed from the wood fibres to the wine.

Varietal: a wine made from a single grape variety. In France the wine must contain 100 per cent of the same variety, but in other countries small proportions of other varieties may be added.

Vintage: originally meaning the annual grape harvest, now meaning a wine from the harvest of a particular year. Each vintage depends on a combination of climatic factors which determine the wine's quality and potential for ageing.

WATER, COFFEE AND TEA

Will you have beer, whisky, gin, other spirits and all the after dinner liqueurs? Due to stringent drink-drive laws, we have become more of a nation of wine, beer and water drinkers with a good measure of soft drinks thrown into the equation. Importantly, water, tea and coffee need to be looked at in depth, as well as the wine.

Water

Water is almost automatically ordered these days, with a huge upsurge in demand for sparkling and still water by customers. A remarkable two billion bottles were bought in 2003.

With profit margins of 500 per cent for most bottled water, some waiters, as directed by their managers, are remarkably skilled at offering 'sparkling or still' as soon as the customer is seated. What will you charge for water?

Although I am always for a fair profit, water pricing has become out of hand. Many restaurateurs charge – wrongly, in my view – exorbitant amounts. This may be an attempt to grab back profits lost by wine and spirit drinkers cutting back. Or it may be sheer opportunism. I would urge restaurateurs to think again as it smacks of out and out greed and will be recognised as such.

A scam – yes, I see it as one – is to charge for filtered tap water, diners paying up to £4.50 for a litre which costs the princely sum of 10 pence. Or a reported scandalous £2.50 per glass.

Is this hospitality? No. Nor do you wish to be seen as a soft touch. Find your profits elsewhere or it could undermine customers' confidence in your restaurant.

Coffee

Coffee is so important for your restaurant. In previous chapters I have urged the necessity of either hiring or buying a good espresso machine to offer espresso, cappuccino, latte, americano and all the other coffees ending in o.

People's expectations are such in today's restaurant market that good coffee is the norm either after a meal, with a meal, before a meal or instead of a meal. It is, to lovers of good coffee, the crowning glory to the end of a meal. Make it work for these aficionados in search of the best.

If you agree with my words about water greed and the signals sent out by charging preposterous amounts, you will recoup by offering a prime commodity: fabulous coffee – but at a reasonable price.

In order to achieve this, the following points are best adhered to:

◆ Have an excellent coffee machine which you either hire or buy.

◆ Make doubly and trebly sure staff know how to operate it. The company will help you with this, but don't lock yourself into a long contract with a machine supplier.

- Experiment with coffee, sourcing good suppliers.

- Grind beans for the best-tasting coffee.

- Have the right cups and saucers to show off your coffee. They may be sourced from the company that hires you the machine. Or buy appropriate cups and saucers. Dainty or 1970s squat, canteen-like cups are not suitable.

- If possible, go on coffee courses to understand the art of coffee.

- Market your coffee well.

◆ TOP TIP ◆

Teas are on the increase in popularity. Do offer quality ones including peppermint and other flavoured teas. Please don't charge overly for a teabag and some hot water if these hot drinks are offered after a meal. It could harm your business.

But, if you are running a tea room or café, you must charge accordingly. The space taken up by customers – and time – must be taken into account. At a recent visit to a reasonably smart London restaurant, two of us were charged £3.50 each for a peppermint tea bag dunked in hot water after a meal. No matter what the overheads are, this is unacceptable in my book.

Other drinks

You will, of course, be stocking your bar or, in the absence of one, an area of your restaurant, with spirits, beers, liqueurs and soft drinks. Have the right type of glasses on adjacent shelving, ice, lemon and other bar accoutrements such as corkscrews, wine coolers, ice buckets. Also have cleaning materials to keep the bar clean and tidy and clean tea towels for polishing glasses.

TRADING STANDARDS GUIDELINES FOR SELLING ALCOHOL

The pricing of all food and drink must be made clear to customers. Have a price list. If you do chalk your food and drink up on boards, make sure they are easily seen and are legible.

The price list should include:

- The price.

- The quantity, for example, 25 ml of gin or ½ pint of beer.

- The price for each quantity. If the price of a double whisky isn't the same as two singles, then show both prices.

- Include VAT in the price.

Where the price list should be displayed

This depends on the way the food and drink are served. Where customers pay for food and drink before consuming it – at the bar or elsewhere – you must display the price list where food and drink are ordered.

If the price list can't be read from where the orders are taken, you should display a price list at the entrance to the eating area.

In restaurants, the price list should be displayed in the window or in the reception area so that customers can see prices before they enter the restaurant.

Obviously, this is not practical for most restaurants, these guidelines perhaps applying to vast chain bars and restaurants. A drinks list is the usual type of information given to the customer with the menu, and this seems to suit establishments and Trading Standards officers alike.

However, weights and measures should be strictly adhered to. Despite Europe (which includes Britain of course) being metric, even Trading Standards are not going totally metric as you will note in the following:

- Beer, lager and cider, except when mixed with other drinks, can only be sold draught in these quantities:
  - ⅓ pint, ½ pint or multiples of ½ pint.

- Gin, whisky, rum and vodka: unless they are sold in cocktails, they may only be sold in these quantities:

- – 25 ml, 35 ml or multiples of these quantities

- – old imperial measures (gills) cannot be used for the sale of any spirits.

◆ A notice which is easy to read by customers must make it clear which quantity applies: in quantities of 25 ml or multiples therof.

◆ The same quantity must apply in all the bars of pubs, restaurants or cafés.

◆ Optics or thimbles for measuring purposes must be stamped and where customers can see them being used.

◆ If you run out of a particular drink, you must remove it from the price list as soon as reasonably practicable.

◆ Wines by the glass must be sold in the following quantities:
  - – by the bottle
  - – by the glass in 125 ml, 175 ml or multiples of these quantities
  - – these quantities must be made clear to customers either in a notice or on every wine list or menu
  - – by the carafe in 250 ml, 500 ml or 1 litre quantities.

This is not an authoritative interpretation of the law and is intended for guidance (courtesy of the West Sussex County Council). Contact your local council's Trading Standards officers for further guidance.

12

The Day to Day Running of Your Restaurant

You have achieved your goal of owning a restaurant and it's time to open your doors to the paying public. You've put all that hard work into locating good premises, and sorted out the finances, the environmental health officer and other legalities. The furnishings and fixtures look just as you had hoped and planned and the kitchen has passed the test, working its way through the menu with aplomb.

Marketing has been worked at assiduously and you want to test it.

You are staffed, the produce has been sourced and bought, you've had your opening party and the word is out on the street: **you are open**.

THE DAILY PATTERN

First, look at what the day to day running of the restaurant is like. This chapter outlines some front of the house bare essentials. A small restaurant kitchen's day's work is outlined, which may help to set you on course. It will hopefully give you a picture of what is in store.

For every restaurant there is a pattern, no matter how many hours they are open, to deal with preparation, serving, clearing away and paperwork. Most restaurants start work from one to four hours before service, depending on the type of food served.

If it's a restaurant with little of the food actually prepared on the premises, then one hour will usually suffice but, if the food is cooked from scratch and done to a high standard, the kitchens will be busy from early morning.

Planning

A well-run restaurant thinks ahead with its planning. If it doesn't it will be chaotic and the business will suffer.

In the morning, first thing, a well-run kitchen's chefs will check the stocks (if they haven't done so and ordered the night before) making sure the menu's offerings can be adequately covered. Then ordering of perishable goods takes place, and dry goods are also checked and ordered if necessary.

If there is a market nearby that offers quality produce, the chef may go or delegate staff. This is the ideal but, sadly, isn't normal practice in Britain.

Preparation

Preparation of the food begins. A menu of bought-in food will require less advance cooking, but salads and other garnishes may be prepped to enhance the food.

A restaurant that will serve only food freshly cooked to order can prepare certain dishes to a point. This is called the *mise en place* (literally, the putting into place) – preparing all the raw material as far as possible, the assembly taking place when the order is received.

These preparations include soups, stocks, sauces, terrines, patés, boning and trimming meat and fish into portions and, increasingly, stews and daubes made with rabbit, chicken, beef, lamb and vegetarian ingredients. These form the bulk of the morning's preparation with smaller tasks to fulfil before the kitchen staff reassemble for the evening's work.

Vegetables, garnishes and other smaller kitchen tasks follow, as well as a rest, a break and a staff meal before the restaurant is open.

◆ TOP TIP ◆

All of this preparation is for speed of food delivery. Don't underestimate the time it takes!

Division of labour

In small kitchens there may be only one chef, or a chef and commis chef. In larger ones the kitchen is divided into parties or sections for each part of the menu, which may include starters, sauces, meats, fish, grills, vegetables, salads, larder work and desserts.

Each section, when orders come through, will prepare its part, the final assembling of the food perhaps done by the head chef who will always check it before it leaves the kitchen. This is called **the pass**. The food will also have its final check against the order, to see if it matches, before being taken to the table by waiting staff.

This is where the head chef shines. Can he or she generate the energy, help to create the vital teamwork and keep everything running smoothly?

Clearing up

When the last orders begin to trickle through this is the time when the clearing up begins in earnest, although keeping a tidy, hygienic, clean kitchen during service is absolutely vital. Items not used are labelled and stored away or thrown out. No sense in keeping wilted rocket or parsley.

If you are running an all day and evening food service restaurant the menu will be a simpler one. But all the steps – cleanliness, clearing up, keeping a tidy kitchen, a watch on perishables – must be adhered to.

Once the kitchen is back to its pristine state, staff can be released for a break before the next session. Or management might release staff gradually, the first one to leave being the first one back on duty to start the evening's preparation.

FRONT OF HOUSE

Taking bookings: first impressions count

Your bookings book is by the phone on the bar or at some accessible place in the restaurant. Each day should have a separate bookings sheet or date. Have a plan of the restaurant at the front of the book so that staff can identify table numbers. In restaurant-speak, the number of seats are referred to as 'covers'. Ensure that there is enough space in the bookings book for the following:

◆ Time of booking.

◆ Number of people booked in.

◆ Table booked (if applicable) – a window table may be asked for.

◆ Contact telephone number (if people ask why, it is for several reasons: if a booking needs to be changed or cancelled for any reason and, if a no-show or late, to be able to contact them).

◆ Any requests (disabled/special diet/birthday surprise cake and Champagne) or smoking or non-smoking.

A good restaurant staggers the bookings for the sake of the kitchen and the smooth running of the restaurant. But there will always be people who turn up late for their booking who have neither contacted you, nor been contactable by you. This can create a log jam and they may have to wait in the bar, should you have one, until a table becomes available. Explain with tact. Offer them a menu, a drink (but not on the house unless the booking mistake was yours).

The booking sheet could also have the name of the staff member who took the booking in case there are any queries.

Repeat back the booking to the customer to make doubly sure that the details are correct. Obviously, if a customer turns up and you have no record of the booking, or it has been recorded on the wrong day with the wrong information ('I said a table of four, not two'), you may have lost that customer forever.

Staff may be instructed to finish the conversation on the phone or in person with the customer with 'Thank you for your booking and we look forward to seeing you.' Little courtesies such as this one can only give confidence to the customer that this is a caring, polite restaurant.

◆ TOP TIP ◆

A good manager and staff know how to fill a restaurant. They need to know whether table ten is going to be free in two hours and if people coming in are regulars and always like to sit at table ten. Regulars need that extra looking after – and by name.

Staff should also be aware of people with communication difficulties, either when booking a table or taking an order. They should speak directly at the customer so that the face can be seen clearly. Speak normally but more distinctly. Listening attentively to all customers is A Good Thing.

Welcoming customers

When customers come into the restaurant, and if all staff are busy, the manager (if around), or another member of staff, should at least smile a welcome and say 'I'll be right with you.' To ignore customers on entry will not win them over. They may feel unwelcomed and leave.

When dealing with a customer, staff should make it a one-to-one transaction. It is very rude to ignore a customer or deal with them haphazardly or in a distracted way. Deal with one customer at a time. Give them your full attention and you will be appreciated.

Attention to detail is one of the most important issues to get right in the restaurant business.

Preparation of service

Your preparation may vary for a more formal restaurant or if you have a more casual restaurant, but many of the requirements remain the same. In other words, be prepared. This is the front of house *mise en place*, the preparation of service.

Check the booking diary for reservations. Allocate tables to customers (if applicable). Check staff rota and staff present. Go over the menu with staff *before* and not during service. **Waiting staff can make the difference between a good restaurant and a great one.** Do they know what is in each dish and can they explain them to customers? Check that staff look the part and that they have washed their hands before starting work.

Menus

◆ Make sure the menus and wine/drinks lists are clean and complete. Discard any dirty or stained ones.

◆ Has the specials board been agreed with the chef and is it written up clearly?

◆ See if there are any items not on the menu and make sure all staff know what is 'off'.

Bar

Check that:

◆ The bar area is tidy and functional.

◆ The ice and lemon are in place, and white wine bottles replaced in the chiller.

◆ Red wine has been replaced in bins or racks.

◆ There is a good stock of water, soft drinks and beer.

◆ The espresso/cappuccino machine has been switched on and is pristine.

Housekeeping

Check that:

◆ All the housekeeping has been done satisfactorily: loo paper, clean loos, bins emptied, tables set properly, chairs wiped and dusted, any dead flowers thrown out and replaced by fresh ones.

◆ The cleaning materials are ready for wiping tables.

◆ Salt and pepper containers are filled.

◆ If using trays for service, that they are clean.

◆ Cutlery drawers are filled.

The respect given to the manager/owner by the front of house staff should be the same as between kitchen staff and chefs. And the other way around. They are two teams working in parallel. There must be a good working relationship and communication between these two groups of people.

Building up trust

Customers come in. Service has started. Now the administration of making out bills, making sure there is enough change and cashing up at the end of service is to be taken into account.

If the kitchen is behind with the orders, the chef must inform waiting staff so that they in turn can reassure the customer that they haven't been forgotten.

Ensure that waiting staff introduce each dish to the customer, rather than just putting it down without so much as a glance. They are not going to be impressed. Explain what the dish is. 'Braised shoulder of lamb with rosemary, potatoes and greens' is far better than 'lamb'. It's a courtesy thing.

Service

If the tables are set up for four, two, six, eight or any number, and if all places are not taken, the entire setting or settings must be removed.

Rules of service haven't changed much over the decades, with women being served first, all food served from the left and removed from the right. No plates are cleared until everyone has finished eating. Clearing away must be done with the minimum of fuss, clatter and skill. Once the main course has finished, salt, pepper, bread, butter must be cleared too. This is noted and appreciated by customers.

There will always be something to clear. Staff must be eagle-eyed and remove anything dirty to the kitchen or washing up area. While tidying up after a busy service good staff keep an eye on the customers who may want another coffee, the bill, or to ask a question.

◆ TOP TIP ◆

Never be the kind of restaurant whose staff are so eager to sell another bottle of wine but are never around when the customer wants to pay the bill.

The manager must be aware of all tables. Is there one still waiting for a first course for half an hour? Deal with it. Calmly. A good manager is aware of who is eating, how long they have been waiting and if there is a problem that needs solving.

After lunchtime service

Repeat the whole housekeeping, bar, menu, staff process over again. Include in this checking on the menu and the specials board and for any changes for the next food service.

Tables are laid for the next service, the bar re-stocked, menus checked for cleanliness.

Cash is counted and reconciled with the bill totals and another float added to the system. This is particularly important after every meal service, and after every changeover of staff, so that errors can be identified and discussed with the staff member in question.

If you have a restaurant which serves food throughout the day, the process needs to be continually updated.

During a lull, it's time to keep up with the paperwork, the bookkeeping, staff hours, invoices, letters of confirmation to a customer for a function and other necessities. Management and chefs may also be conducting staff interviews, which should be put in the diary for either mid-morning or mid-afternoon. Or all of these may be taken over by management not involved in service.

◆ TOP TIP ◆

Those new to the business may not wish to take a break during sessions. It will do you the world of good to get some fresh air, a change of scene, a different thought process during that all-important lull between lunch and evening. This applies to all staff and is important.

THE KITCHEN

Depending on the size and nature of the restaurant, the start of the day is a movable feast. As a restaurant chef/owner for a 28-cover restaurant I was responsible for the cooking, ordering, the *mise en place* and organising the staff. The restaurant was open from Tuesday lunch to Sunday lunch, and my then husband was in charge of front of house.

As someone once remarked, 'sleep is like rat poison. After a while you get immune to it.' Yes, you do. But an afternoon cat nap can do wonders. Or that's what you do on your day off. If you don't have three children.

A typical day at Soanes Restaurant for eight years

I start my day at 8.30, ready for service at noon. I am aided and abetted by two in the kitchen, Mrs O who does just about everything else, and Jenny who plates desserts and doubles up as a waitress. She is joined by other waiting staff on weekends and busy nights.

The menu changes seasonally, with no specials board. I start on prepping stocks, soups, pastry and terrines, the items that require longer cooking and prepping. My menu consists usually of five starters, five mains and five desserts with an artisan cheese board. *Time to check the deliveries which may start coming in anytime after 8.30 am.*

◆ TOP TIP ◆

And I mean check. Go through the order to see if it is complete and if the produce is of excellent quality. Return any produce that isn't acceptable with the van driver. Or if it's spotted later, call the supplier.

In larger kitchens there are ordering sheets, stock sheets, staff personal information, kitchen equipment maintenance, records of fridge temperatures and the *mise en place* sheets in place for more control. In smaller ones, these steps may be less formal, particularly in one-man-band operations. In all kitchens, chefs have a notebook or, increasingly, computer for recipes and ingredients and when certain dishes were put on the menu. The head chef's management skills must be on a par with cooking skills and menu development.

I either ask Mrs O to label and store deliveries or, if it is a slower day, I do it just to have a good check on freshness and stocks. Mrs O is also in charge of cleaning and may be sorting out the storage room, cleaning the restaurant or putting a pile of tea towels and kitchen whites on to wash. She is a gem and much loved and appreciated.

◆ TOP TIP ◆

Start calling companies if deliveries are late (they could jeopardise lunch service) or if produce isn't up to scratch. As my restaurant was in a small town in the country, deliveries from London came twice weekly only, local produce daily if required (see chapter on sourcing for a fuller picture).

Mid-morning: prep sauces, desserts and peripherals like dressings, making sure I have enough produce to cover an unexpectedly busy lunch period or devise other dishes to put on if I think the more popular dishes may all go.

◆ TOP TIP ◆

If not very busy don't even think of this step as it may result in wastage. But always have some quick to prepare dishes up your sleeve with the produce in stock, should the need arise.

By late morning, lunchtime staff arrive, the rolls are baked, the butter put into dishes. Bookings are checked. All vegetables are now ready for both lunch and dinner service and stored away. We all sit down to lunch and a chat before service.

Lunch

Up the path come the first customers who are greeted in the conservatory and bar overlooking the South Downs. Drinks here first and orders taken or, if they are in a hurry, they go straight to the table and order.

Lunch is in full swing, orders being put on pegs in strict rotation. Vegetables are cooked to order in the Hobart steamer, the chargrill put to use for fish or calves' liver, a beurre blanc having its butter cubes whisked in, the salmon and tarragon terrine sliced and garnished, salads dressed just before being served, a chocolate pithiviers in the oven to be finished off and glazed then served with an almond sauce.

The swing door whisks open and shut between kitchen and restaurant. Laughter and the babble of voices come through to the kitchen where, surprisingly, there is little bumping into one another as we tend to anticipate our moves. Waiting staff know better than to get around the stoves anyway!

The cheeseboard is rescued from its chilly home (the law is an ass when it comes to being able to have cheeses at room temperature), five cheeses plated onto a rectangular dish with suitable breads and oat cakes in tow. The coffee machine hisses in the corner with yet another espresso emerging. Mine.

Service over

When service is over, the kitchen is left pristine. Staff leave for the afternoon, returning at 6 pm for a 7 pm start. I check the fridges for produce, make a list on the board of prepping to do and have a few hours off if it isn't a busy evening or a weekend.

At 6 pm the rolls go in to be finished off, bookings are checked, the stock pots strained, cleaned and put away to leave more room for a busy evening's cooking. When staff arrive, a meal is either eaten or, quite often, they eat off the menu after service at a high kitchen table and we go through the day and discuss anything that went wrong – or right! Or improvements that could be made, adjustments to the menu that might improve the sale of certain dishes and any feedback that emerges.

Showtime

But, before this meal, it is showtime! The orders come in, the plated food goes out garnished and followed by suitable vegetables, desserts plated and served. Chicken breasts spatter their skin fat on the range, steam rises from the mussels, the door between the pass flaps in and out.

That wonderful pressure is on to do 28 starters, main courses and desserts, the layering of the thought processes – which dish is cooked when – as complicated as attempting to play a game of tag with 28 people simultaneously.

Just four more orders to go. 'Please don't have the scallops with pea puree, I've only got one more portion!' They don't, going for the chargrilled lamb with a garlic sauce, roast sea bass with a sesame prawn crust, a wild mushroom risotto and beef fillet with Dauphinoise potatoes.

Shut down

Then suddenly the restaurant is empty apart from regular customers chewing the fat with front of house. The kitchen is scrubbed down, rubbish put out and staff check their rota after their meal.

At nearly midnight staff rev up their cars or motor bikes in the car park and leave, the South Downs beyond lit up by a flash of lightning. It is beautiful. And quiet again. But there is still the ordering to do on the phone, some more checking of produce and then the kitchen lights go out for another day.

WHY DO IT?

Why do people do it? It's a buzz. For that and being creative, giving pleasure, and working, learning and growing as a team. Trying out new ideas. Meeting an interesting crowd. It is mostly sheer fun, it's pure theatre, it's a living and it sure beats working in an office.

Of course it is very different in a large kitchen or in another type of restaurant. I only outline my experiences. Treble, quadruple the covers, the staff, the produce, the size of the organisation and it has to be even more scrupulously and meticulously worked out. And so well disciplined to work properly. Some see it as organised chaos. Some as a thing of beauty.

13

Customer Relations and Being a Customer

Running a restaurant is mainly about the responsibilities the restaurant has towards its customers and staff. But what about the responsibilities of the customer towards restaurants? This chapter outlines both of these obligations and, with a foot in both camps, how to put yourself in your customers' shoes.

Handling customers is a skill that will come with the running of a restaurant, if you don't already possess it. It may be useful to have some points laid out beforehand to help you on your way.

As hotelier and restaurateur Kit Chapman (Castle Hotel and Brazz chain), in his *An Innkeeper's Diary*, reports: *our clients are getting more demanding and difficult, not less. Attention to detail is the mantra we chant and success relies on our ability to respond to their wishes.*

A carefully planned, well organised, perfectly well executed party is no guarantee of a satisfied customer. Any number of complex human ingredients may intervene: mood, prejudice, fear, personal taste, class snobbery, social inadequacy, megalomania, a row with the wife, the death of a pet. (Take your pick.)

We're in the mind-game – part psychology, part clairvoyance. We're in the business of making magic.

How true. And how succinctly put if a trifle depressing. However, it does help to understand what the hospitality business is about and what can be achieved if taking on board the complex nature of people.

CUSTOMER SATISFACTION

Good management recognises the decline of customer satisfaction, the symptoms being:

- Increasing complaints about the staff.
- Increasing complaints about the food or produce.
- More accidents taking place in the restaurant due to poor maintenance.
- Arguments between staff which affect the atmosphere.
- Poor morale in the business.
- Breakages or shortages of equipment resulting in staff being unable to do their job properly which, in turn, affects the customer.
- High turnover of staff.

Customers may also be aware of the lowering of standards by staff:

◆ Do they smile at customers?

◆ Are they courteous towards customers?

◆ Do they say please, thank you, excuse me?

◆ Management might ask themselves if the staff member is in the right job or if there is a problem to be solved.

◆ Do they greet customers or congregate around the bar, ignoring them?

HANDLING COMPLAINTS

If a problem comes up and the customer makes a complaint the following may be of help:

1. Don't interrupt the customer.

2. Never lose your temper.

3. Don't take it personally (hard, I know!).

4. Don't argue.

5. Don't place the blame on another person.

But:

1. Do apologise for the specific complaint.

2. Do move into a quieter area with the customer if possible to discuss the complaint, so as not to upset other customers.

3. Do re-state the complaint to show you understand the nature of the problem.

4. Do agree that the customer was right to bring that particular problem up (within reason, of course!).

5. Act in a quiet, professional manner.

6. By keeping your voice low the customer's anger can partly be dispelled.

7. If you feel their complaint was justified, then do offer to take the offending dish off the bill if this was the problem and replace it if applicable.

8. If it was the service, a glass of wine, a bottle, free coffees all around might suffice.

PROMOTING CUSTOMER SATISFACTION

This summing-up list highlights factors which make up a good restaurant experience:

- The welcome, décor, ambience.

- The booking (if appropriate): has it been taken properly?

- The location of the table.

- The menu and drinks list (contents and cleanliness of the lists).

- The order being taken and identifying who the host is (if appropriate).

- Availability of the food on the menu.

- The speed and efficiency of service.

- The pleasantness and courtesy of the staff.

- The staffs' unobtrusive waiting skills and attentiveness.

- The ability to attract the attention of staff.

- Other customers' behaviour (eg rowdy, shouting, drunk, overuse of mobile phones).

- How complaints are handled.

- Method of presenting the bill and collection of the payment.

- The departure and how this is handled (ignoring departing customers, being off-hand or the opposite).

Putting yourself in your customers' shoes: attention to detail

Watch your staff to see if they welcome customers. Discuss this with your staff if you see any shortcomings. Perhaps they are all around the bar, talking to one another rather than keeping an eye on the customers.

Sit at all of your tables and look around you.

- Firstly, are the chairs comfortable and suitable for the type of operation you run? If you are sitting for a length of time over a meal of merit you don't want to squirm uncomfortably in your seat.

- Secondly, would you really want to sit next to a loo door, a swinging kitchen door with all the clatter of a busy kitchen, by a draught from the front door or by coat hangers with coats brushing against your chair and maybe you?

- Are the tables big enough for bottles of wine, water, serving dishes, candles, flowers, cutlery, napkins, oversize plates? If not decide what you are going to do about it.

- Are the tables clean and wiped down properly before a customer sits at one?

- Are the surroundings clean? Are those cobwebs and dirty marks I see on the ceilings, walls and skirting boards?

- Why are these dirty, torn menus being given to customers?

- Why are there streaks on the cutlery and the glasses?

- Why are these flowers past their sell-by date and not replaced?

- Why is the bar looking as if a bomb has hit it?

- Why haven't all those dirty glasses on the bar been moved to the washing up area and out of full view of customers?

- Have the staff washed their hands or is that a dirty thumbnail I see on a plate that is to be served to a customer?

- Are waiting staff, when serving the food, telling the customers what the dishes are in some detail and not just saying 'fish, paté, soup, meat'?

- Why are the tables not being cleared properly and quickly?

- Why is a staff member's shirt hanging out, and shoes not cleaned and polished?

- Why are the windows dirty or smudged?

- What are staff doing hanging out by the bins in full view of the restaurant and having a cigarette break?

- Why is the music so loud when I return to the restaurant after a break? Decide if this is the restaurant's policy or whether the staff are upping the volume while you or the manager are away.

- Why are the toilets not cleaned and well stocked with toilet paper, soap, paper towels? Analyse why this rota has not worked. Or maybe there is not a rota in place.

- Why are there grubby marks on doors to the toilets, the kitchen, the entrance doors?

- Why is the kitchen in a mess? Why isn't it being cleaned properly?

- Why is this food uncovered on a kitchen counter?

- Why are the bins overflowing?

- Why has this tired lettuce leaf been put on a plate as a garnish?

- Why am I eating a chicken breast that tastes of nothing or is of poor quality? Consider whether the chef is not ordering well and with care, and if the cooking is up to scratch.

- Why is this stale bread being served to customers?

- Why is the wine not being sufficiently chilled?

- Why does this dish look as if it's been thrown onto the plate rather than being prepared and plated with due care and attention?

- Why are people waiting for their drinks or food? Is there a hold-up in the kitchen? Or don't I have enough staff on duty?

◆ Why is the coffee from that very expensive coffee machine I so carefully sourced not being made or served properly? Consider whether staff need more instruction on how to make good coffee.

◆ Are staff working as a team? In the kitchen? In the restaurant? As a whole?

◆ How have staff handled the bills and their payment?

◆ Are staff saying goodbye in a pleasant manner? Are they sullen or smiling?

A long list, but well worth taking the time and effort to go through. If you find that some points are justified, address them.

BEING A CUSTOMER

Is the customer always right? No, of course not. We live in somewhat boorish times with some pretty unpleasant behaviour taking place in public places.

But, equally, there are many delightful human beings out there who will be charmed by your restaurant, your staff, your food and the ambience you have created. They are the ones who will flock to your restaurant, for the greater part. And you will be charmed by them.

And, hopefully they will remember to:

1. Turn up in time for a booking and respect your business, taking into account that the system of the restaurant (putting pressure on the kitchen) might suffer if they are late.

2. Call the restaurant if they are going to be late.

3. Contact the restaurant if numbers in their party are up or down as you simply can't magic chairs or tables out of thin air if the booking changes.

4. Contact the restaurant to cancel a booking.

5. Keep their drinking at a decent level and not get drunk on your premises.

6. Complain politely if a problem occurs.

7. Not treat staff as servants, but see them as professionals and equals.

8. Not complain over trivia.

9. Say thank you for good food and service. This is music to staff, chefs and management's ears.

TOP TIPS

Tips from established restaurateurs to those contemplating opening a restaurant and newcomers in the business:

◆ If starting, beware of your own *naîveté*.

◆ Select staff who wish to make catering their career rather than those just in it for the money.

◆ Don't select staff who have been through catering college and think they know everything. In this business you never stop learning.

◆ Treat your customers as you would good friends being guests in your own home.

◆ Be realistic and straightforward, avoiding all pretentiousness.

◆ Don't use your imagination just for the sake of seeming imaginative.

◆ Only cook what you understand and cook well.

◆ Buy in small quantities, frequently, so that your food is always fresh.

◆ If you mix a variety of ingredients from East and West know what you are doing, as it could result in a total mishmash of flavours with customers running screaming from the premises. Pickled ginger with mashed potatoes doesn't work as a pairing.

◆ Get an accountant!

◆ A good review is worth thousands of pounds in advertising.

◆ Word of mouth is the best advertising. For every satisfied new customer, another five to ten people will hear of it from that customer.

- Be good humoured.

- Have good interpersonal skills.

- Have good feet!

- Be a mind reader.

- Honestly know your food and wine.

- Enjoy company and really like people.

- Hire staff carefully: they need to fit in personally as well as being efficient.

- Create a happy kitchen atmosphere. Don't have chefs who cook in anger. Customers will pick it up.

- The best food is soul food and you can't cook in chaos or that sweaty, macho, it's-hell-in-here-but-we'll-get-the-job-done atmosphere so beloved of catering regiments. Ever notice women rarely cook like that?

- Cynicism and marketing always show. The best restaurants are expressions of the people who create them.

- Don't forget dining room improvement, service and menu upgrading. Regular customers like to see the place they know and love being maintained and improved.

- Believe in what you are doing and look at the long term.

- Be consistent.

- Raise your prices very slowly.

- Do not try to please everyone.

- Know your strengths and weaknesses.

- When starting your business keep your price below the competition and your quality above.

- It is important to be able to say no.

- Develop your palate. Always try new tastes and keep up to date.

- Never serve food you do not taste.

- In good restaurants there are no VIPs. All your customers are VIPs.

- Being a restaurateur can eat up family life. Safeguard your family by delegating and spending more time with them. This is vital.

- Service is not servility.

- Encourage children to eat all types of food in your restaurant. They are the next generation.

- It is a mistake to presume that good food alone makes for a good restaurant.

- Know your market and who you are catering to, then design your menu, premises, ambience, pricing, service, style.

- Regard cooking and service as of equal importance.

- Lead by example, by training all staff to respect their work and the contribution they make to the restaurant.

- Avoid pushy advertising and salespeople.

- You need to be strong in mind and body, for restaurant demands are great.

- Be loyal to good suppliers and pay them on time. They will go out of their way to help you in the future.

- Never make drastic changes to the menu but change them gradually and within seasons. Your customers might be put off by too drastic a menu change.

- Be patient with staff. You will rarely have perfect staff so look to their positive points and hope to improve their bad ones. See them blossom.

- Getting the right financial and accounting advice from the beginning is the difference between a viable and non-viable business.

- Keep up with your paperwork. If you can't, hire a bookkeeper.

- Set-up costs are frightening. Don't be put off. You have to spend money to make money.

- Kitchen equipment can be bought second-hand or leased.

- Market research is important. There is no point in offering your style of cooking or restaurant if there is no demand.

- It's a good idea to specialise, eg organic food or seafood.

- Never rest on your laurels.

- Don't get one wine company to do your full list.

- Don't be under-financed as the pressure will force you to work all hours.

- Take good breaks to restore the brain and for inspiration.

- There are customers out there who are just out to give a restaurant a hard time. Grit your teeth and be so revoltingly pleasant that they will be eating out of your hand.

- Attention to detail. It's the little things that matter.

- Staff must be constantly reminded, cajoled, kicked and generally encouraged to get it right.

- Don't chop and change your opening hours as it confuses the hell out of people.

- Spread your bookings. The restaurant that allows all its customers to arrive at 8.30 pm is courting disaster.

- Happy bosses and happy staff make happy customers.

- Chefs should only become chefs when they develop their own intellect. Too many young chefs are influenced by fame and fortune, and don't necessarily have the passion and heart.

- Ignore all the above if you're an accountant thinking of setting up a restaurant as an investment – you probably know it all already!

- Despite everything, it is a most fascinating business.

Postscript

This descriptive piece summed up an Edinburgh Festival mask show, Familie Floz:

Ristorante Immortale is everywhere and nowhere. It is heaven and hell. It is the restaurant that never opens but never closes, has a staff that serves but never sleeps and it is where you can go eat your fill but still go back for more.

It is a metaphysical culinary Fawlty Towers where dreams and nightmares, comedy and pathos collide. It is like a waiter in a great restaurant eager to please and makes you feel like a valued customer.

Should you decide to open a restaurant I hope that the information, experiences and practicality – aided and abetted by common sense – in this book have helped you on your way to an informed decision.

May you open – and close when you wish – and may you have many valued customers who return for more and more of your rewarding hospitality.

I wish you good fortune.

Glossary

STAFF

Chef de partie Literally 'head of a team'.

Commis chef The most junior chef, learning his or her trade.

Demi chef de partie Literally 'half' – fewer responsibilities.

Executive head chef In charge of a large restaurant or restaurants, hotel restaurants or a catering company.

Kitchen brigade The name given to kitchen staff as a whole.

Head chef In charge of the kitchen, staffing, menus, suppliers.

Kitchen porter The underpinning member of the kitchen who washes up, preps vegetables, is in charge of rubbish.

Sous (under) chef Head chef's immediate number two and capable of carrying out head chef duties in absence of head chef.

USEFUL COOKING TERMS

Al dente An Italian term meaning 'to the tooth' in the cooking of pasta with a resistance to the bite.

Bain-marie Deep pan of hot water in which dishes to be cooked are placed prior to being put in a low temperature oven. Also a large water tray on top of the stove to keep sauces like Hollandaise and custard warm without overcooking or spoiling.

Bake blind Baking pastry cases without filling, but lined with foil and ceramic or metal beans then baked prior to filling being added.

Blanch/refresh Fast-boiling vegetables for a few minutes then refreshed in cold water to keep their colour. A possible holding point for further cooking. Can also be for whitening meats or fish to remove any trace of impurities. Also for skin removal of nuts, tomatoes, peaches and peppers.

Chambrer To bring cheeses to room temperature for maximum flavour.

Clarify butter Removing the milky residue by gently heating butter, then either pouring it through muslin or pouring it carefully into a container without disturbing the residue.

Confit Traditionally, confit only applies to lightly salted duck or goose cooked slowly in its own fat and then preserved in this fat. When ordered, the meat is then roasted. Nowadays, it is widely misinterpreted on menus, sadly demonstrating the restaurateur's basic lack of knowledge.

Decant Pouring liquid – wine, meat juices etc – carefully from one container to another without disturbing the sediment.

Deglaze Adding liquid – stock or wine – to a pan in which meat has been roasted, then boiled to reduce, and whisked into the concentrated juices and crusty bits to form a gravy which is then strained and seasoned.

Gratin A preparation of food cooked in a shallow dish with a sauce, and finished in the oven or under the grill to produce a crust thanks to the addition of breadcrumbs or cheese.

Julienne Cutting vegetables into strips or matchstick shapes.

Jus Very often misinterpreted, the jus is short for 'jus de viande' (juices of the meat). Nowadays it is a sauce halfway between a gravy and a complex sauce made from stock, wine and other seasonings.

Lardons Small strips of bacon, salt pork or pork fat blanched then sautéed.

Monter Whisking cold cubes of butter into a sauce to thicken it. Can also mean whisking egg whites lightly or stiffly.

Reduce Reducing a stock or sauce by evaporation over a high heat until it reaches the wished-for consistency. This intensifies the flavours.

Relax Relaxing meat after cooking allows the re-balancing of juices and enhances the colour of red meat.

Roux A mix of fat, usually butter, and flour which is whisked in little by little to thicken a sauce. It must be cooked for quite a while to eliminate the taste of raw flour.

Sautéing Literally 'to jump' (French). The shallow frying of smallish pieces of food in an open pan with fat to brown the meat.

Supreme The skinless breast and wing of chicken or game such as pheasant. It can also be applied to fish fillets to glamourise them on restaurant menus.

Sweat Cooking food over a gentle heat, usually in oil and/or butter, until softened but without colour.

Terrine An ovenproof, usually loaf-shaped dish for cooking patés with or without a pastry crust.

Tornedos A small, round, usually expensive steak cut from the thickest part of the fillet. Trimmed of all sinew and fat.

Tourner or **to turn** Cutting vegetables into olive, almond or barrel shapes.

Wilt Usually a green leaf or herb with a few drops of water from its washing, turned with tongs in a hot pan until just wilted but retaining its colour.

MISCELLANEOUS

Corked wine Wine that has been tainted by a contaminated cork.

Mirin Japanese sweet cooking wine made from fermented yeast rice grains.

Miso A savoury paste of cooked soya beans with grains, yeasted grains and sea salt which is fermented for one or two years.

Quinoa (pronounced 'keen-wha') Gluten-free grain similar to bulgar wheat and used instead of rice, couscous or bulgar for those on a gluten-free diet.

Useful Contacts

British Chambers of Commerce www.britishchambers.org.uk

British Hospitality Association www.bha-online.org.uk (020) 7404 7744

British Institute of Innkeeping www.bii.org (01276) 684449

Business Debtline: (0800) 197 6026

Business Eye in Wales www.businessconnect.org.uk (08457) 9697 98

Business Gateway (Scotland-Lowlands) www.bgateway.com (0845) 609 6611

Business Link (0845) 600 9006 or www.businesslink.gov.uk

Companies House www.companies-house.gov.uk (0870) 333 3636

Equal Opportunities Commission www.eoc.org.uk (0845) 601 5901

Federation of Small Businesses www.fsb.org.uk

Food Standards Agency for A–Z of who to contact (from alcoholic drinks to waste issues) (020) 7276 8000

Food Standards Agency for publications www.food.gov.uk (0845) 606 0667

Food Standards Agency site for caterers www.food.gov.uk/cleanup

Health and Safety Executive www.hse.gov.uk (08701) 545500

Henrietta Green's Food Lovers' Fairs www.foodloversfairs.com

HM Customs & Excise National Advice Service (0845) 010 9000

Highlands and Islands Enterprise (Scotland-Highlands) www.hie.co.uk

Home Office helpline re overseas workers www.ind.homeoffice.gov.uk 0845 010 6677

Imported Food Helpline (020) 7276 8018 (Food Standards Agency)

Inland Revenue www.inlandrevenue.gov.uk

Landlord disputes www.bdl.org.uk

National Association of Farmers' Markets www.farmersmarkets.net

National Minimum Wage Helpline (0845) 600 0678

New Employers' Helpline (0845) 607 0143

Papworth Trust www.papworth.org.uk

Part-time workers' regulations www.dti.gov.uk/er/ptime.htm
Performing Rights Society www.prs.co.uk
Rare Breeds Survival Trust www.rare-breeds.com
Restaurant Association www.ragb.co.uk (020) 7831 8727
Small Business Service www.business.link.gov.uk
VAT helpline (0845) 010 9000
W.I. Markets www.wimarkets.co.uk

See Chapter 10 for further contacts

Bibliography

Small Business Co.UK; The Restaurant Association of Great Britain; *Caterer and Hotelkeeper*, www.foodreference.com, www.datamonitor.com; *Eating British 2004*; *British Cheese Directory 2003*; *The British Regional Food and Drink Guide*; *The Observer*; *Observer Food Magazine*; *Evening Standard*; *The Guardian*; The *Times*; Food Standards Agency; Performing Rights Society; The Papworth Trust; The Home Office; The Inland Revenue; HM Custom and Excise; The Immigration Service; Department of Trade and Industry; *In Business* (BBC Radio Four), *Yellow Pages*, Federation of Small Businesses, British Chamber of Commerce, Walnut Tree Inn, Monmothshire, Brake Catering.

Beckett, Fiona *Wine by Style* (1998) Mitchell Beazley.

Chapman, Kit *An Innkeeper's Diary* (1999) Weidenfeld and Nicholson.

Erdosh, George *Start and Run a Catering Business* (2001) Self-Counsel.

Gray, Rose, Rogers, Ruth *River Café Cook Book Green* (2000) Ebury Press.

Grigson, Sophie *Sophie Grigson's Herbs* (1999) BBC.

Hughes, Diana and Golzen, Godfrey *Running Your Own Restaurant* (1986) Kogan Page.

Johnson-Bell, Linda *Good Food Fine Wine* (1999) Cassell.

Ladenis, Nico *My Gastronomy* (1987) Ebury Press.

Lehrian, Paul *The Restaurant* (1953) Practical Press.

Lillicrap, Dennis, Cousins, John, Smith, Robert *Food and Beverage Service* (1998) Hodder & Stoughton.

Little, Alastair *Keep It Simple* (1993) Conran Octopus.

McKenna, John *How To Run A Restaurant* (1998) Estragon Press.

Parker, Ken *Buying and Running a Small Hotel* (1992) How To Books.

Parkinson, Andrew, Green, Jonathan *Cutting It Fine* (2001) Jonathan Cape.

Riley, Michael *Managing People* (2000) Butterworth Heinemann.

Roux, Albert, Roux, Michel *New Classic Cuisine* (1983) Macdonald.

Weller, Lyn *Health and Vitality Cookbook* (2000) Harper Collins.

Whyte, Stewart *Starting and Running a B & B* (2003) How To Books.

Wood, Martin *Leith's Guide To Setting Up A Restaurant* (1990) Merehurst.

Index